customising
clothes with
embroidery

15 fun projects to inspire you to upcycle
the clothes you already own

customising clothes with embroidery

15 fun projects to inspire you to upcycle the clothes you already own

CONNIE MABBOTT

Photographs by Jesse Wild

WHITE OWL

This book is dedicated to my mum, who has been my number one fan since the day I brought home my first handmade Easter card at primary school.

First published in Great Britain in 2021 by
PEN & SWORD WHITE OWL
An imprint of Pen & Sword Books Ltd
Yorkshire – Philadelphia

Copyright © Connie Mabbott, 2021
@_conniesworld

ISBN 9781526784469

A CIP catalogue record for this book is available from the British Library.

Group Publisher: Jonathan Wright
Series Editor and Publishing Consultant: Katherine Raderecht
Art Director: Jane Toft
Editor: Katherine Raderecht
Photography: Jesse Wild
Styling: Jaine Bevan

Printed and bound in the UK, by Short Run Press Limited, Exeter.

Pen & Sword Books Ltd incorporates the Imprints of Pen & Sword Books
Pen & Sword Books Limited incorporates the imprints of Atlas, Archaeology, Aviation, Discovery, Family History, Fiction, History, Maritime, Military, Military Classics, Politics, Select, Transport, True Crime, Air World, Frontline Publishing, Leo Cooper, Remember When, Seaforth Publishing, The Praetorian Press, Wharncliffe Local History, Wharncliffe Transport, Wharncliffe True Crime and White Owl.

For a complete list of Pen & Sword titles please contact:
PEN & SWORD BOOKS LIMITED
47 Church Street, Barnsley, South Yorkshire S70 2AS, England
E-mail: enquiries@pen-and-sword.co.uk
Website: www.pen-and-sword.co.uk
or
PEN AND SWORD BOOKS
1950 Lawrence Rd, Havertown, PA 19083, USA
E-mail: Uspen-and-sword@casematepublishers.com
Website: www.penandswordbooks.com

contents

Introduction 06

Techniques & tips 10

Materials & equipment..................... 14

CHAPTER ONE: BASIC EMBROIDERED LETTERING

1. Simple Initial T-shirt 18

2. 'Wild' Jumper.................................22

3. 'Smile' T-shirt.................................26

CHAPTER TWO: FREE-MOTION EMBROIDERED PATCHES

1. Monstera T-shirt.............................32

2. House Plant Initial Jumper............36

3. Snake Clutch Bag........................42

4. Embroidered Fluffy Coat 48

CHAPTER THREE: FREE-MOTION DIRECT ONTO GARMENTS

1. Simple Floral T-shirt......................60

2. Floral Blouse 64

3. Pink 'Peachy' Midi Skirt................68

4. 'Be Kind' Blouse..........................72

5. Cutwork Denim Top......................76

6. Daisy Cardigan 82

7. Celestial Crop Top 88

CHAPTER FOUR: DESIGNING AN EMBROIDERED DENIM JACKET

1. Embroidered Denim Jacket...........94

Stockist Directory 110

About the Author............................. 112

introduction

I'm Connie - I'm in love with all things embroidery and run my own embroidered fashion brand called Connie's World. Growing up I always loved creating things with fabrics and wanted to work in fashion. However, living in a remote area of Wales, that career path just wasn't offered at my school or college. I was determined to follow my dream so, as soon as I was old enough, I left home to study Textile Design at Birmingham City University. It was at university that I discovered my love of embroidery and I specialised in the technique during my second year. Without knowing it, I was on a path that would soon lead me to the fashion job I had always dreamed of. After I graduated, I worked in a few jobs that involved making embroidery pieces but I couldn't help making my own embroidery designs on the side and, in 2018, I founded Connie's World and started selling my own designs online. Although the T-shirts and jumpers I sell online are brand new, ethically and sustainably sourced garments which I then embroider in my studio, I still love upcycling and updating my existing wardrobe with unique embroidery designs, and browsing charity shops and second-hand markets for hidden gems!

Throughout this book I will share the hints, tips, and techniques I've learnt through my own embroidery journey and help make learning how to customise your clothes with embroidery as simple as possible. Free motion embroidery can be quite a difficult technique to get the hang of – it requires lots of patience and practice - but once you've got the hang of it you can create beautiful results. My tips will prevent you making the mistakes that commonly occur when starting to learn free-motion embroidery. I aim to make your embroidery journey easy and stress free. Rather than this being a book full of step-by-step tutorials showing you how to make an exact copy of every project, I want to inspire you to come up with your own designs. By sharing my inside knowledge of the best kept secrets in free-motion embroidery, you'll be in the perfect position to get started.

In a world dominated by fast fashion, making us think we should get rid of old items of clothing to make room for new purchases, it's liberating to give your pre-loved garments new life by upcycling and embellishing them. Just because something has lost its appeal, or has a small hole or a stubborn stain, doesn't have to mean it has to be thrown away and replaced with something new. Cover up those little faults with beautiful, unique embroidery and you'll transform those tired threads into your new favourite statement piece. Best of all, you can wear your new creation proudly, knowing you have something one of a kind, handmade and special.

HOW TO USE THIS BOOK

All the projects in the book are made using a mixture of straight foot sewing and free-hand motion embroidery on a regular domestic sewing machine, with the occasional addition of hand embellishments and finishes. Starting with simple ideas that can be completed in an afternoon to get you warmed up, we'll move onto more complex, detailed projects that will keep you busy for weeks. Finished pieces like tops, denim and accessories will inspire you to start decorating your own clothes and filling your wardrobe with totally unique, upcycled pieces that no one else owns.

The upcycling embroidery in this book spans a range of abilities from beginner to expert. I'll start with how to create initial ideas and designs, work through the process and then guide you through to the finished pieces. If you're new to using sewing machines for embroidery, start with the simpler ideas before tackling the bigger, more complicated projects.

All the garments used for the projects in this book were either already owned by me, or purchased from charity shops and second-hand or vintage markets. Most of the items I have used are pieces that many of us already have in our wardrobes - jackets, T-shirts and jumpers - or can be found in most second hand shops on your local high street. There should be plenty of ideas to get you going without having to invest in lots of expensive new clothes.

You will find the basic instructions for all the techniques used throughout the book in the techniques and tips section; refer back to them whenever you need to refresh your memory. Be patient, practise your skills and most importantly, have fun with your own projects!

techniques & tips

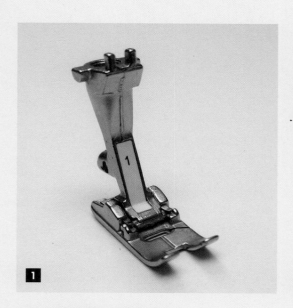

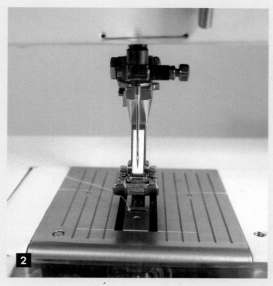

STRAIGHT FOOT SEWING

Straight foot sewing is the simplest way to
use your sewing machine. You will need your
machine set to straight stitch (a brand new
sewing machine will usually already be set up
like this). Make sure the straight foot is on the
needle **(Fig. 1.)** and that the feed dogs (the
small teeth under your needle and foot area)
are up so that they pull the fabric through the
needle **(Fig. 2.)**. How you do this can be
different depending on what model of sewing
machine you are using, so check the instruction
manual if you are unsure. Select your stitch
length depending on your model of sewing
machine and you're ready to go. On the
Bernina 1008s sewing machine used in this
book, all these settings can be found printed on
the right of the machine. Always test your stitch
length on some scrap fabric before committing
to using it on a piece of embroidery to make
sure you're happy with how it's sewing.

ZIG-ZAG SEWING

You can create zig-zag stitches by changing the
width of your basic straight foot sewing stitch.
Most sewing machines offer a stitch width of up
to 5mm. For a regular sized zig-zag, the stitch
length and width should be set to approximately
two to three millimetres. This is a great technique
to appliqué patches on garments. You can
also use zig-zag sewing for satin edgings by
increasing the stitch width, and reducing the
stitch length so that the needle will zig-zag
wide from side to side and only move forward
a fraction between each stitch. For many of the
projects in this book where a satin edging is
used to outline, the stitch length is set to 1mm,
and the width to approximately 4mm.

techniques & tips

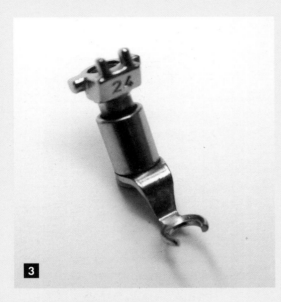

3

FREE-MOTION SEWING

This technique is achieved by lowering the feed dogs so that they don't catch the fabric and try to drag it whilst sewing. If you forget to do this, you will feel a slight pull when trying to free-motion sew. You will need an embroidery foot for this technique **(Fig. 3.)**. Embroidery foots can look different depending on the machine you use, however, they tend to be rounded at the bottom. Stitch width and length will need to be set to zero for this technique. It is always best to use an embroidery hoop for free-motion sewing, as they are designed to pull the fabric taut which helps prevent puckering. Free-motion sewing is a way of embroidering by using your hands to move the fabric in the embroidery hoop around under the moving needle to create your design. If you don't use a hoop you run the risk of the fabric bunching up - and you'll also be moving your hands quite close to the needle.

SATIN STITCH FREE-MOTION

A technique for the advanced, this is a way of getting the beautiful effect of satin stitch with free-motion embroidery. It is achieved by free-motion embroidering with the feed dogs down and the stitch length set to zero, but with the stitch width set to as large as you want the satin effect to be. This action is much slower than the previous techniques, as the needle moves from side to side to create the long stitches. Press down hard on your foot and glide the fabric slowly so that the zig-zag is tight and creates a beautiful satin effect. Use this technique around the edges of your design for a neat edge, and then fill in the design by moving the hoop side to side at the same time for a shaded effect. This is more difficult to master than using regular free-motion sewing, but if you learn free-motion satin stitch you will achieve incredible results.

HAND STITCHING

Hand sewing is a useful skill even when your focus is on free-motion embroidery. Throughout this book, some of the projects may require hand work for appliquéing on embroidered patches, beading or small hand finishes. Your needle should be threaded with any cotton thread (silky embroidery threads are likely to fray and/or snap with hand sewing) and knotting it on one end. Try to leave about 10cm of thread hanging from the needle on the non-knotted end to prevent it from falling out when stitching. Secure your knot before you begin by making a few stitches at the start point before continuing your hand sewing or beading. Push your needle through the fabric (or fabrics) and pull through

techniques & tips

slowly so that the thread follows. To avoid the thread knotting on the way through, try and hold it taut with your other hand so it doesn't bunch up as it goes through the fabric.

HAND BEADING

When beading, you will need the thread to be a little thicker to keep the beads secure, as they can often get caught on things. Cut a piece of cotton thread twice the length you need in the same colour as your beads or your fabric. Thread a beading needle, bring the two ends of your thread together and make a knot in them so you are using doubled up thread when stitching. Start from the back of your piece and create a few small stitches to secure the thread, before attaching beads on the front side of your design. When the beading is complete, create a few tight stitches on the back of the piece to secure it before cutting the loose threads away. You can stitch each bead on individually, or thread multiple beads on at once and stitch them together. It all depends on the effect you are trying to achieve.

ESSENTIAL STRAIGHT FOOT SEWING AND FREE-MOTION TIPS:

■ Always use a backing fabric. Tear-away backing is best so it can be removed once the embroidery is complete, but be careful when tearing it away!

■ If you're unsure how long your stitch or how wide your zig-zag stitch will be when using the straight foot, test on some scrap fabric first to make sure you're getting the result you want before starting on your design.

■ Draw your design on water-soluble film and pin it to your fabric. You can also use a vanishing pen to draw your design straight onto your fabric. I prefer using film as it helps to stabilise the fabric and will keep the drawing marked out until you remove it. Water-soluble film can also be removed easily.

■ Different types of thread can require different levels of tension, so test your thread out on a scrap of fabric first to ensure your tension is right. If you can see the bobbin thread coming through to the top, the tension is too tight. If the bobbin thread makes knots on the underside, it's too loose. You can change the tension on both the upper thread and the bobbin thread.

■ Trace your design out on the fabric before using a satin stitch with your straight foot or filling in with free-motion to fix the film or backing in place on the fabric.

■ Try to use thin needles on your machine because the thinner your needle, the more detail you can create. This does mean, however, that they are more prone to breaking so be careful when using thin needles with thick fabrics and designs heavy with stitching.

■ Attaching an extension table to your sewing machine can really help when using a free-motion embroidery technique. Without one, you may find your hoop rocks either side of the bobbin case.

■ Wooden hoops are fine for free-motion embroidery, however using a spring hoop can be easier. You can keep the hoop small which maintains the tightest tension, and reposition it around the fabric with ease without having to tighten or loosen any screws.

materials & equipment

USEFUL TOOLS AND MATERIALS

■ A selection of different coloured threads to make your vibrant embroidery projects pop

■ Both a straight foot and a free-motion foot for your sewing machine

■ Tear-away backing fabric/embroidery stabiliser

■ Water-soluble film and/or an air erasable vanishing fabric pen

■ A pair of small, sharp scissors suitable for cutting embroidery threads

■ A pack of thin needles for your sewing machine (recommended size 70/10)

■ Any scraps of fabrics you may have

lying around – these can be for testing on, or patterned to use as part of your design

■ Felt for patches in any colour of choice (must be colour fast)

■ Pins for securing materials together

■ Embroidery hoop (recommended – spring embroidery hoop)

■ Iron-on interfacing/Bondaweb

■ Thermoweb Peel'N' Stick Fabric Fuse – for attaching embroideries to accessories

■ Hand sewing needles – for hand finishes and beading

■ Selection of beads (optional)

basic embroidered lettering

The easiest way to update pre-loved items or cover small stains or holes in clothing is to use a patch. Many shops sell ready made iron-on patches, but the designs can be quite uninspiring. What better way to update your wardrobe than to make your own patches? This chapter introduces the beginner techniques you will need to learn to make your own patches, using mainly straight stitching techniques.

simple initial t-shirt

You will learn: Basic alphabet patches using straight foot sewing.
Start your upcycling journey with this simple Initial T-shirt. In this project we will use easy-to-work with materials like felt, and a simple straight foot to get you started. You'll also use up scrap fabrics that have been lying around!

Skill Level: Beginner

You will need
- Tear-Away Backing
- Pink Fleece
- Water-Soluble Film
- White T-Shirt (pre-owned)

Equipment
- Sewing Machine (I use a Bernina 1008)
- Straight Foot
- Small Embroidery Scissors
- Pen

Embroidery threads
- Gunold Sulky 1193
- Gunold Sulky 1067
- Gunold Cotty 100 (used for bobbin thread)

Alphabet patches are very simple to make. Simple, plain felt is ideal for the base as it's the right thickness, is very forgiving, holds stitches well and can be found in most craft shops. With a sturdy base fabric, almost any fabric can be used to add colour and pattern. For this project, a soft pink fleece was used for the base colour of the 'A'.

19

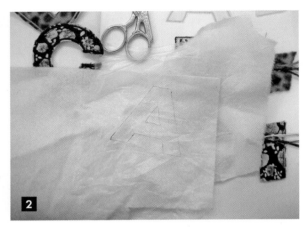

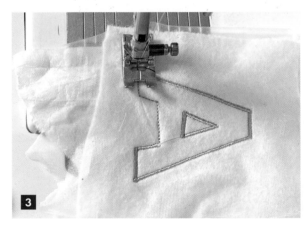

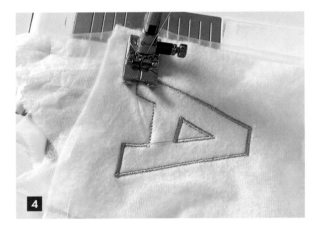

Simple block fonts are the best style of lettering to start with. Choose a font and print out your chosen letters on any home printer, or draw your letters by hand then transfer on to your fabric for stitching.

Alphabet patches are a great way of updating tired pieces of clothing, but they are also a means of using up any scraps of material lying around from old projects. If you use patterned fabrics cut out from old clothes or blankets you can add detail to your letters without spending hours filling in the shapes with heavy, detailed embroidery. For the best results, trace out the letters onto a small piece of water-soluble film with a regular pen **(Fig. 1.)**. Alternatively, mark the letter design straight onto your fabric with

a vanishing felt pen. Next get your fabrics ready to sew. You are making a sandwich of fabrics with the tear-away backing on the bottom, the plain felt base in the middle and the water-soluble film with the letter marked out on top **(Fig. 2.)**. If you are using an extra fabric for pattern or colour, this should be placed between the base material and the film. You are now ready to start sewing.

Sew around the outline of the letter with a straight stitch set to a moderate length to secure the fabrics together and prevent the design from moving when you come to the satin stitch. If you're using an erasable pen, it's also a good idea to get the outline marked out before the pen lines disappear.

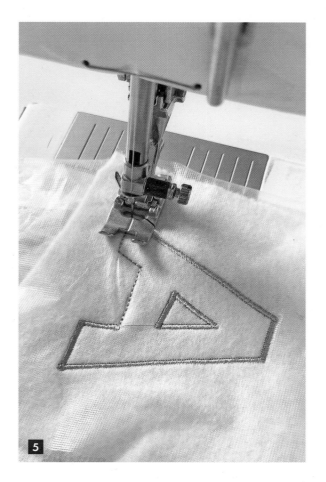

Follow the outline with a close-set zig-zag stitch to create a satin effect around the edges **(Fig. 3.)**, **(Fig. 4.)**. Set the length of the stitch to approximately 0.5, and the zig-zag to no less than 2.

I advise testing your settings on a scrap of fabric first to make sure you get your desired effect. After working around the whole letter in zig-zag, the extra stabiliser materials (tear-away backing and water-soluble film) can be pulled away and the patch cut out.

The cut-out patch can then be sewn onto your chosen item of clothing. Use a piece of tear-away backing on the inside of the garment and zig-zag stitch your patch on to the clothing **(Fig. 5.)**. Using

the tear-away backing material on the inside of the garment where you are applying the patch helps prevent the fabric from puckering if it's thinner than the patch. Try not to push the fabric through the sewing machine. The satin effect zig-zag stitch is a lot slower than a regular straight stitch and if you force the fabric it can create gaps around the edges of your patch. Be patient, use your hands as a guide and let the feed-dogs do their work.

In the example **(Fig. 6.)**, a contrasting colour thread has been used to apply the patch in order to highlight the design. Once you have zig-zag appliquéd all around the edges of the letter patch, the piece is complete and ready to wear!

'wild' jumper

You will learn: Creating words and phrases with letter patches.
Take your letter patches to the next level and form words to create statement garments like this 'Wild' Jumper. This method is the same as the Initial T-shirt but introduces you to playing around with pattern and form with lettering.

Skill Level: Beginner

You will need
- ▪ Tear-Away Backing
- ▪ Leopard Print Fleece
- ▪ Water-Soluble Film
- ▪ Pink Sweatshirt (pre-owned)
- ▪ Denim Jacket (pre-owned)

Equipment
- ▪ Sewing Machine (I use a Bernina 1008)
- ▪ Straight Foot
- ▪ Small Embroidery Scissors
- ▪ Pen

Embroidery threads
- ▪ Gunold Sulky 1056
- ▪ Gunold Poly 61913
- ▪ Gunold Cotty 100 (used for bobbin thread)

In this project you will take using patch letters to personalise your clothes to the next level, by forming a word, name or even sentences. This project uses leopard print fleece as a base for the word 'Wild'. Print out or draw the word before tracing it onto a piece of water-soluble film large enough to cover all of the text. Follow the steps for individual letters in the Initial T-Shirt to stitch out the word, name or phrase.

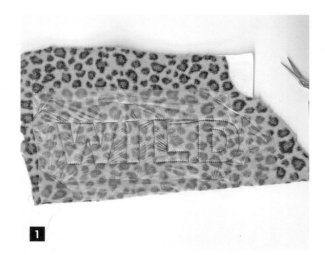

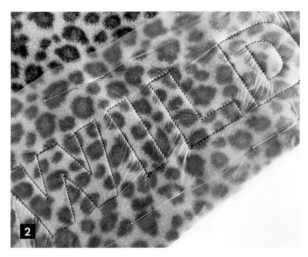

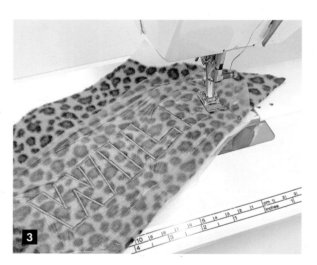

Do all the base stitching for the whole word first, before moving on to the zig-zag satin stitching **(Fig. 1.)**, **(Fig. 2.)**. Keep the fabric sandwiched between the water-soluble film and tear-away backing when using the zig-zag setting to stitch the satin stitch edging, especially when using delicate materials or fabrics with a high pile **(Fig. 3.)**.

Using patterned fabrics or bold colours is a great way to uplift a plain garment. Experiment with a decorative fabric and toned down threads. Play around with design placement too; you can create

an arch out of the letters, combine different styles of lettering or mix the colours of the letters **(Fig. 4.)**.

Pinning the patches to the garment with some tear-away backing on the inside helps to keep the composition in place. For extra security, you can attach the letters using iron-on adhesive or Bondaweb to ensure the patches don't move when you are sewing them down. Think about using a different colour thread to satin stitch appliqué the patches onto the garment – contrasting and bright colours work well with nudes and natural tones and help to lift the

lettering **(Fig.5.)**, **(Fig. 6.)**.

Words can be used to upcycle all kinds of garments - think about using lettering on the back of a denim jacket or on T-shirts or jumpers. Position the patches on your garment first in various compositions to see how they will look when stitched down **(Fig. 7.)**, **(Fig. 8.)**. Combine the letter patches with other customisable embroidery ideas throughout this book to make a completely unique item of clothing.

EXTRA TIPS & IDEAS FOR APPLIQUÉ LETTERING

■ You can hand stitch your letters. Stop raw edges from fraying by sewing a tight zig-zag stitch around the edges of the letters before sewing them onto your garment.

■ If the base fabric is an easy-to-use material that doesn't fray, like felt, you can use most fabrics on top to add pattern or colour. Coloured felt can be used with no top fabric; however, watch out, as felt is not always colour-fast.

'smile' t-shirt

You will learn: Cursive wording with free-motion sewing.
This project introduces the embroidery foot, which is used for a more free style of embroidery. It requires more practice than the simple straight foot but once mastered can create beautiful cursive lettering results.

Skill Level:
Improving Beginner

You will need
- Tear-Away Backing
- Plain White Felt
- Pink Fleece
- Water-Soluble Film
- Pink T-shirt
  (pre-owned)

Equipment
- Sewing Machine
  (I use a Bernina 1008)
- Straight Foot
- Small Embroidery Scissors
- Pen
- Spring Embroidery Hoop

Embroidery threads
- Gunold Sulky 1193
- Gunold Sulky 1511
- Gunold Cotty 100
  (used for bobbin thread)

This project takes us to the next level by using more decorative fonts. Design your own font or print out your text onto water-soluble film. When working with more rounded, cursive lettering, use the embroidery foot and an embroidery hoop to stitch around the outline of the letters. Use a free-motion

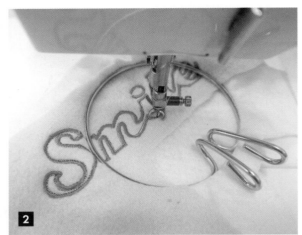

stitch to clearly mark out your stitch line and secure the layers of materials together. Make sure both the stitch length and width is set to zero, and the feed dogs are down (feed dogs are the little teeth that feed your fabric evenly through your sewing machine. Read more in Techniques & Tips).

For the satin stitch outline, re-attach the regular straight foot and return the machine settings back to the same zig-zag settings you used for the basic letter patches in the previous projects. Put your feed dogs up, use a stitch length 0.5, width approximately 2.5. Test your stitching on some scrap material if needed before

using it to outline the text **(Fig. 1.)**.

Think about using different fabrics for decorative elements, or using contrasting stitch colours to make the outline stand out against your chosen materials. These patches are perfect for upcycling plain T-shirts or jumpers with pieces of scrap fabric from old, unwanted clothing, off-cuts in fabric shops, blankets, curtains and any other soft furnishings you don't want to throw away.

For an added bit of detail, go back to using the embroidery foot to add a line of stitching inside the satin outline **(Fig. 2.)**. This isn't an essential step, but

5

it can be used to add an extra colour if the fabric you have used is quite plain.

Once you have added all your chosen detail and stitching elements to your text, the topping and backing fabrics can be removed and the piece cut out **(Fig. 3.)**. Cut it approximately 0.2mm from the outline stitch. Pin it in place on your chosen garment, using backing fabric on the inside of the garment to stabilise the fabric. Appliqué using a zig-zag stitch **(Fig. 4.)**, **(Fig. 5.)**.

After trimming around the wording, you can stitch your word onto any garment using the same satin zig-zag technique. Placing tear-away backing on the inside of the item will help prevent puckering, particularly when appliquéing onto lightweight materials.

TAKE IT FURTHER
Create entire quotes or phrases using this technique, using any style of fabric - from plain or floral, animal print or geometric. You can combine this technique with a free-motion design in the centre if you'd prefer to create your own pattern, or don't have the fabric in a pattern you like.

free-motion embroidered patches

Patches are a great way to learn free-motion embroidery. As you'll be mainly working with scraps and cheap materials, if something goes wrong with the design or you create a hole (much more likely with thin fabrics used for T-shirts), it doesn't matter as much as it would should you be working directly onto the garment itself. The materials I recommend for embroidered patches tend to be thicker, sturdier materials that are much less likely to puncture.

monstera t-shirt

You will learn: Basic shaped patch appliqué.
Basic motifs like this Monstera shape can be created with a straight foot if you're not comfortable with using a free-motion foot. This project guides you through how to create simple, yet beautiful, shapes and designs using easy methods.

Skill Level:
Improving Beginner

You will need
- Plain Paper
- Iron-On Interfacing
- Tear-Away Backing
- Green Cotton Fabric
- Striped Pink T-shirt (charity shop buy)

Equipment
- Sewing Machine (I use a Bernina 1008)
- Straight Foot
- Small Embroidery Scissors
- Pen

Embroidery threads
- Gunold Sulky 1177
- Gunold Sulky 1287
- Gunold Cotty 100 (used for bobbin thread)

An easy way to begin embroidering basic motifs onto garments is to start with the simple straight stitch. In this project I upcycle a charity shop find with a simple Monstera leaf design. Using fabric scraps to create the general shape and colour of the design not only provides an outline to follow, but also adds structure and density to a thin t-shirt material, which helps make it easier to stitch into.

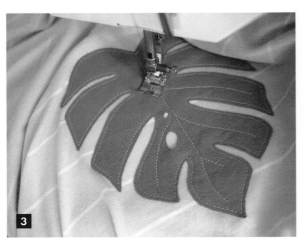

Most materials can be used for this technique, including those that are prone to fraying. Applying some iron on interfacing to the back of the fabric will help reduce fraying and provide an area to trace the design onto **(Fig. 1.)**.

Draw out your design onto a simple paper stencil. You can then use your stencil to draw the outline of the design onto the interfacing on the back of your fabric, before cutting out and placing onto your garment. At this stage, take into consideration any stains or holes you might be trying to cover up and make sure that these are well hidden by the design **(Fig. 2.)**.

With some tear-away backing on the inside of the garment, use a straight stitch to appliqué the motif onto the garment. Add detail using different shades of thread or contrasting colours that complement your design **(Fig. 3.)**. Use a zig-zag stitch around the outline of the design to hold the edges down.

Once you're happy with the level of detail, the tear-away backing can be carefully removed from the inside of the garment **(Fig. 4.)**. If, after removing the tear-away backing, you want to continue working on the design by adding more stitches, it's as simple as reattaching a fresh piece with some pins before

5

continuing to embroider.

This piece has two thread colours, but can be made with multiple shades and colours to create more detail and depth to the image. Consider how many times each line is stitched over and which elements you want to stand out more. Incorporating more lines will add detail and the opportunity to mix more colours, shadows and highlights into your design **(Fig. 5.)**.

TIPS TO EXPAND ON THIS IDEA

If your design is quite complex, try using free-motion embroidery rather than straight foot sewing – it's

much quicker and freer. Straight foot sewing is great for beginners and for getting perfect, straight lines but can be time-consuming, especially with designs that require a lot of direction changes.

Make a feature out of raw edges that are prone to fraying by skipping the iron on backing and the zig-zag edging. Be sure to do a double stitch line around the shape though to keep the edges secure! This will give a loose frayed effect that looks particularly striking.

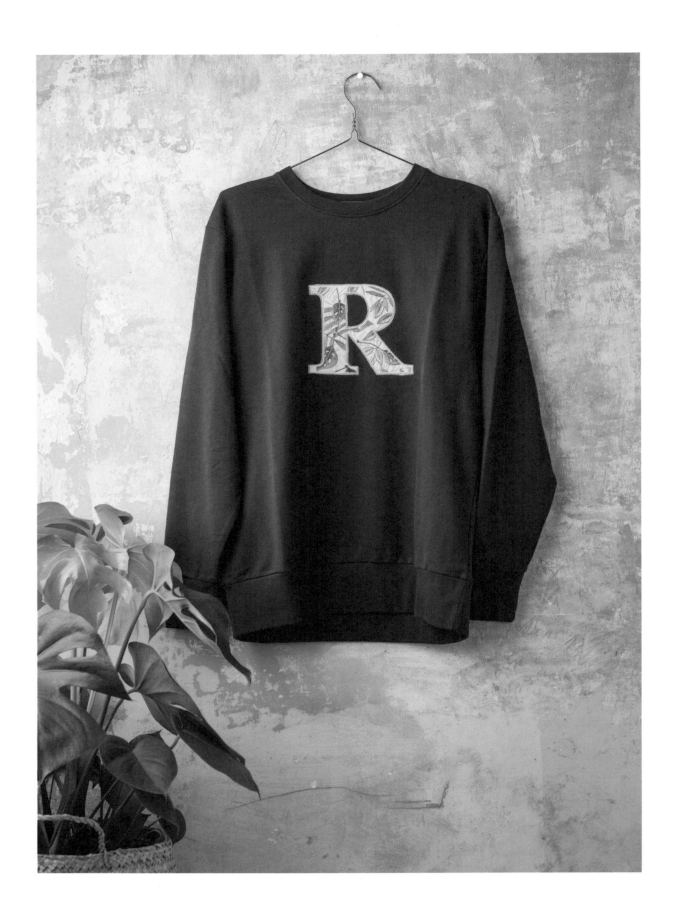

houseplant initial jumper

You will learn: Decorating statement initials with free-motion.
This project combines simple alphabet patches with free-motion. Starting with free-motion and finishing off with the strong outlines, this is a fantastic way to get colour and motifs inside simple shapes without using patterned fabrics.

Skill Level:
Intermediate

You will need
■ Tear-Away Backing
■ Plain White Felt
■ Light Pink Cotton Fabric
■ Water-Soluble Film
■ Navy Blue Sweatshirt
 (pre-owned)

Equipment
■ Sewing Machine
 (I use a Bernina 1008)
■ Straight Foot
■ Embroidery Foot
■ Small Embroidery Scissors
■ Paper Scissors
■ Pen
■ Spring Embroidery Hoop

Embroidery threads
■ Gunold Sulky 1115
■ Gunold Sulky 1119
■ Gunold Sulky 1077
■ Gunold Sulky 1170
■ Gunold Sulky 1287
■ Gunold Sulky 1177
■ Gunold Sulky 1051
■ Gunold Sulky 1272
■ Gunold Sulky 1174
■ Gunold Cotty 100
 (used for bobbin thread)

If you are confident with straight stitching and using the zig-zag feature on your sewing machine to create satin edges, then the next stage is to try decorating your letters or motifs with beautiful free-motion designs of your own. In this example, a foliage design was created from sketches of indoor plants. Start, as in previous projects, by tracing out and making basic letter patches from your own designs or printed out on your computer.

37

1

2

I like to create a whole page of patterns and then choose my favourite section to use inside my letters. To save time, draw out your design inside the lines of each letter you will be embroidering. Planning colours in advance of sewing by adding them to your drawing and choosing the thread shades to match will help to make it easier to create the results you want from your embroidery. This leafy pattern was designed using paint for the colour and detail with pencils and an inky pen **(Fig. 1.)**.

If designing a sheet full of beautiful patterns and choosing your favourite section is your chosen method, make a stencil out of some plain or scrap paper. Make your stencil either by drawing your own letter or printing one out and then cutting it out. Use this stencil to place over your sheet of patterns to find the best looking section **(Fig. 2.)**.

Once you are satisfied with the design, trace it out on some water-soluble film. Be sure to include the letter shape as well as the outlines for all the pattern elements inside the letter. Place this onto your chosen fabric – felt works well as it is sturdy and doesn't fray. Consider whether you would like the background plain or coloured. I chose a pink cotton for this project. If you choose a coloured fabric, make sure it is colour-fast or it may run in the wash **(Fig. 3.)**.

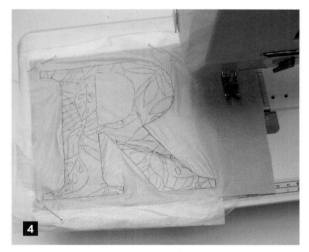

Pin your chosen fabric between the water-soluble film and some tear-away backing and sew them together by stitching around the shape of the letter using a basic straight stitch in a thread colour that either matches the fabric, or the colour outline of your final patch **(Fig. 4.)**.

To embroider the design, the fabric should be framed up in an embroidery hoop. Pull it tight and change your sewing machine settings to the free motion mode and a free-motion foot. Put your feed dogs down and set your stitch length and width to zero (read more about how to free-motion embroidery in 'Free-Motion Sewing' under 'Techniques & Tips'). If you've planned out the colours of your design, you can stitch all the elements in each colour in one go to avoid lots of unnecessary thread changes. This does take planning so don't worry if you can't work this out - there is no right or wrong way to go about which elements to embroider first **(Fig. 5.)**.

It helps to trace out the outline of your motif first before filling in and adding detailing or highlights. If you need to go back to a previous colour to incorporate more detail then do so.
This process can take some time if the design is particularly heavy with detail or consists of a lot of different colours **(Fig. 6.)** but take your time and enjoy

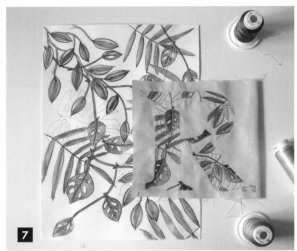

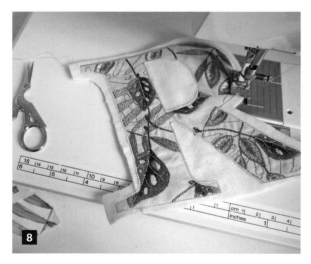

the process **(Fig. 7.)**.

After all your free-motion elements are complete and you're happy with the way it looks, the machine settings can be switched back to the straight foot sewing ready for the satin stitch edging. Put your feed dogs up and set to a short stitch length and moderate width on the zig-zag setting. Trace the shape of the letter you made previously using the running stitch by keeping the line in the centre of the zig-zag **(Fig. 8.)**.

Remove all the tear-away backing and water-

soluble film once you're happy with the finished piece. If the pattern inside the letter is quite detailed, the water-soluble film can be removed completely by placing in some warm water and allowing it to dry **(Fig. 9.)**.

The letter in this example is quite large to allow for lots of space for the detailed design. However, you can make your letters or motifs as big or small as you like! Create names and words, or even one extra large letter to create a statement sweatshirt **(Fig. 10.)**.

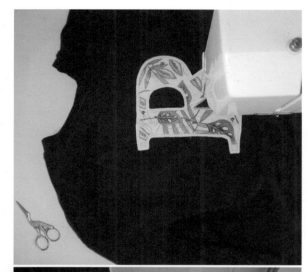

10

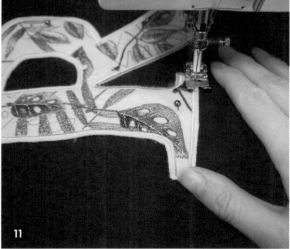

11

The best way to stitch your finished designs down onto garments is, as detailed in Chapter 1, by placing some more tear-away backing on the inside of your garment and using the zig-zag satin stitch technique to attach the patch with an outline. Check the positioning of your patch first by pinning it in place and trying the garment on before committing to the satin edging **(Fig.11.)**.

MAKE IT YOUR OWN

You can use anything as design inspiration - from your favourite TV show or film, to your favourite food! Create a patchwork with scraps of material, embroidering them before stitching the first outline with straight stitch. Aim to make your newly updated item of clothing a complete one of a kind.

snake clutch bag

You will learn: Using free-motion patches on accessories.
In this project you will use the free-motion foot to create intricate embroideries
with layers of colour and detail using a range of free-motion effects. This project
also teaches you how to use patches to decorate heavy materials like leather.

Skill Level:
Advanced

You will need
- Tear-Away Backing
- Plain Black Felt
- Water-Soluble Film
- Thermoweb Peel 'N' Stick Fabric Fuse
- Faux Leather Black Clutch Bag (pre-owned)
- Masking/Washi Tape

Equipment
- Sewing Machine (I use a Bernina 1008)
- Embroidery Foot
- Small Embroidery Scissors
- Older Scissors (for adhesive cutting)
- White POSCA Pen
- Spring Embroidery Hoop

Embroidery threads
- Gunold Sulky 1001
- Gunold Sulky 1005
- Gunold Sulky 1317
- Gunold Sulky 1263
- Gunold Sulky 1301
- Gunold Black 61005 (used for bobbin thread)

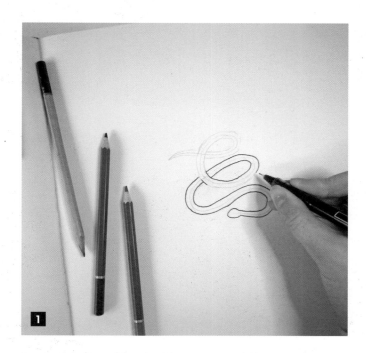

Ever wanted to add embroidery to your old bags and accessories to give them an update, but thought the thickness of the leather might be too tough to get through? No problem. Some leathers are soft and can be stitched into by hand or machine. However, needles leave puncture holes so there is no room for error. Avoid making mistakes by using an adhesive designed specifically for bonding fabrics together.

For this statement clutch bag, the design was inspired by images of red and black snakes. Snakes can be tricky to draw in proportion so I find a clever technique is to draw a quick swirl in your desired shape, and then fill out the lines of the body around it. This method can work for any swirly design, such as vines, foliage or even cursive text **(Fig. 1.)**.

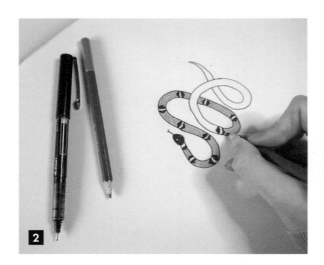

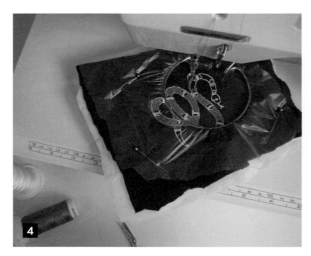

Use your drawing stage to plan out how you want to stitch out your design by using the same techniques with your pen as you plan to use with your needle **(Fig. 2.)**. The black satin areas of this snake were filled in using a zig-zag technique with a black pen, and the red areas coloured in using a coloured pencil to create the swirling effect of the scales.

When using real imagery for inspiration, colour choices come easily as you can simply match your chosen shades to the colours in the photograph or drawing. Having said that, there are no rules when it comes to

colour selection for embroidery! Think outside the box if you want to make your embroideries as original as possible.

When you're happy with your design and are ready to recreate your drawing in embroidery, trace out the design onto some water-soluble film. Use any regular pen if your base fabric is light in colour. However, if you are using a dark base, a dark pen mark can be difficult to see when embroidering. In this case use a white pen so that it shows up against the darker background **(Fig. 3.)**.

Sandwich the base fabric for the patch in-between a layer of tear-away backing and some soluble film marked with the design and pin all three in place together. Frame up inside your hoop and start free-motioning.

The most basic way of using free-motion embroidery is by moving the fabric back and forth to fill in areas with stitch. Use this method if you're a beginner and need practice before moving onto other ways of filling in. For the main red area of the snake, the lighter red thread was stitched in circles across the body by moving the hoop around in very small circular motions whilst stitching to create a 'French knot' effect **(Fig. 4.) (Fig. 5.)**. A darker thread was then used to outline the small circles for the 'scales' effect. This circular free-motion technique also works really well for the insides of flowers **(Fig. 6.)**.

The black elements were embroidered using a satin stitch effect. Set the zig-zag on the machine up to a moderate width and using this to slowly free-motion. Setting the machine to a moderate to large zig-zag whilst free-motion stitching can help to fill in large

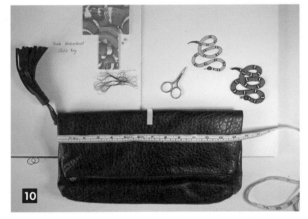

areas of colour more quickly than the usual back and forth stitching. For more help with using the zig-zag setting on your machine for satin effect embroidery, see 'Zig-Zag Sewing' in 'Techniques & Tips'.

After the embroidery is complete, remove all backing and topping fabrics to reveal the design on the patch base **(Fig. 7.)**. For applying patches to thick accessories like this clutch bag, don't cut out the patch just yet. Firstly, cut a sheet of Thermoweb Peel 'N' Stick Fabric Fuse out to cover the whole design plus a few extra millimetres on each side. Remove one side of the paper liner and press the uncut embroidered fabric down onto the adhesive, ensuring that it covers the entire embroidery. You will need some older scissors

to cut out the design with the adhesive attached, as some of the sticking agent may come off on the blades which would ruin a good pair of embroidery or fabric scissors **(Fig. 8.) (Fig. 9.)**.

For precise placement, measure your accessory or garment and place a small piece of masking or washi tape to indicate where you would like it to be positioned **(Fig. 10.)**.

Measuring and marking the piece for placement isn't essential if you want your patches to cover your bag in a more irregular arrangement. First test the position of your design by placing the cut-out patch in your desired location, before gently peeling away the remaining paper liner and placing onto the item,

pressing in place and rubbing to ensure it is stuck well – be sure to press down on all edges too **(Fig. 11.) (Fig. 12.)**.

Once the patch is stuck down, it cannot be removed as the adhesive is very strong and, if you try to move it, it will leave a sticky residue on your accessory so make sure you're confident and happy with your placement before committing to it.

TIPS FOR FREE-MOTION & USING ADHESIVES

Use bobbin thread shades that best match the base fabric colour. For lighter colours, white is perfect. You shouldn't see the bobbin thread coming through to the top layer too much if the tension is right, however if your top layer is quite dark you may see some flecks of white. For darker base fabrics use black, or any cotton, non-embroidery thread that best matches the base colour.

Thermoweb Peel 'N' Stick Fabric Fuse can be used on clothing too, just be sure to read the instructions regarding washing your items afterwards. Consider decorating trainers or leather shoes that look a bit tired and worn, or to adorn purses and notebooks. When using adhesives like Thermoweb Peel 'N' Stick Fabric Fuse do not combine with machine or hand sewing after the fuse has been applied as the needles will become sticky and get stuck.

embroidered fluffy coat

You will learn: Various levels of intricacy in embroidered patches.
This coat is decorated with a range of different embroidered motifs that differ in difficulty to show that simple and easy can often turn out just as beautiful results as something more detailed and difficult!

Skill Level:
Intermediate to Advanced

You will need
- Tear-Away Backing
- Plain White Felt
- Water-Soluble Film
- Pink Satin (Shell Patch)
- Fluffy Borg Coat

Equipment
- Sewing Machine (I use a Bernina 1008)
- Embroidery Foot
- Small Embroidery Scissors
- Air Erasable Pen and Pen
- Spring Embroidery Hoop

Embroidery threads
- Gunold Sulky 1317, 1115, 1056, 1170, 1130, 1023, 1025, 1005, 1074, 0508, 1001, 1168, 1095, 1177, 1174, 1067, 1193, 1194
- Gütermann Sulky 8003
- Madeira Rayon Classic 1320
- Gunold Cotty 100 (for bobbin and hand sewing)

The best way to ease yourself into free motion embroidery is to work with forgiving fabrics and simple designs to start with. Medium weight fabrics work best for beginners, as thin fabrics can be prone to punctures and pucker around the edges if you're not careful, whereas thick fabrics can be tricky to frame up and too dense to sew through and get the detail you want. For these patches, the base fabric I used is just a simple white felt, which can be found in most craft shops and online retailers.

SIMPLE HEART PATCH

Starting with basic shapes like hearts, which have straight and curved lines, is an easy way to start your free-motion journey. Use stencils or cookie cutters to get the perfect shape, or draw your own to embroider from **(Fig. 1.)**.

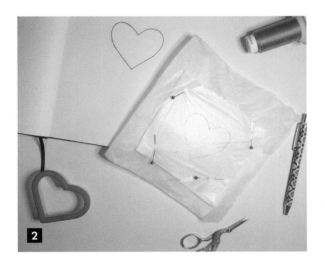

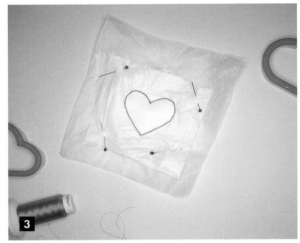

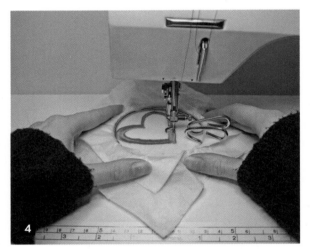

When working on perfectly symmetrical shapes like hearts, be sure that the water-soluble film with the design drawing on it is pinned absolutely flat on the patch base fabric and tear-away backing so that the embroidery doesn't turn out uneven **(Fig. 2.)**. Attaching the embroidery frame can cause the film to move slightly, so keep an eye on it and adjust where necessary. Alternatively, frame the base fabric and tear-away backing before tracing your design (using a cut-out template or stencil) onto the taut fabric so that nothing moves. Note that this will only work if the design area fits within the hoop and can be fully embroidered without moving it around to access all areas.

Use free-motion settings found in 'Free-Motion Sewing' under 'Techniques & Tips' on your machine for this. Put your embroidery foot on the needle and have the feed dogs down and then outline the shape a few times by moving the hoop with your hands before working on the fill **(Fig. 3.)**. Solid shapes can be filled in with regular free-motion, moving the shape under the needle around it to fill in as much as you want, or by adding a satin effect by setting your zig-zag as wide as possible for a 'Satin Stitch Free-Motion' effect, found in 'Techniques & Tips', and

outlining the shape slowly, working your way into the centre gradually one line at a time until the shape is completely filled with the thread colour **(Fig. 4.)**.

Another quick way to achieve a similar result is to include an extra layer of material in the same colour you intend to fill the shape with. Place this fabric between the base and film layers (if using film), and trace the shape a few times before trimming the edges of the top fabric and concealing the raw edges with a simple satin edge stitch using the zig-zag setting.

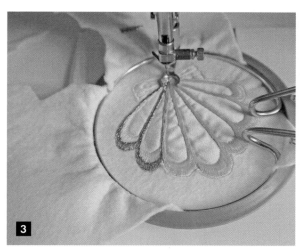

PINK SATIN SHELL PATCH

Using additional fabrics with a patch base can generate beautiful, lavish looking results, especially when using plush velvets or silk-like materials.

Take this shell embroidery, for example **(Fig. 1.)**. After considering a few different designs and selecting the best thread colours to complement a pink satin material, the idea was re-imagined onto the coloured fabric using an air erasable pen. When using air erasable pens, test on your materials first to check it doesn't stay – with a brand-new pen the marks can sometimes take a few days to disappear.

Place the coloured fabric on top of the base patch material – in this case pink satin over white felt, backed with some tear-away backing – and pin together before framing up in an embroidery hoop. As with the heart patch, trace the design a couple of times with a basic free-motion stitch to secure the layers together. When using an air erasable pen make sure the design has been traced before the pen disappears (the older the pen the quicker it will disappear).

The use of fabrics as a fill colour looks most opulent combined with a satin effect stitch to add levels, frame the design, and hide any raw edges. As before, be sure to cut away the excess top fabric before adding

any satin outlines, so that the organic edges can be concealed **(Fig. 2.)**.

For this piece a wide border of satin effect free-motion stitch was added to the curves of the shell in a thread close in colour to the fabric to add depth and layers to the design. The entire shape was then framed using a shiny gold thread for extra opulence **(Fig. 3.)**. Use the zig-zag setting on your machine to your advantage - combine a layer of perfect satin effect stitching with ordinary free-motion for dramatic results with lots of shading.

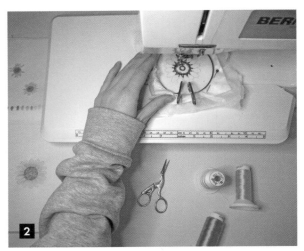

SMALL DETAILED SUNFLOWER PATCH

When moving onto more detailed, difficult projects it helps to start small so as not to overwhelm yourself with a large piece of embroidery. By easing in with a single basic flower no bigger than the palm of your hand, the finished piece should take no longer than an hour depending on your skill level which makes it feel more achievable if you are keen to improve on your basic free-motion skills.

This sunflower was designed using dried and pressed flowers as drawing subjects created with a mixture of paint and pencil drawing mediums.

When using water colours for painting embroideries, it helps to dot a small mark of colour onto a scrap piece of paper or a page in your sketchbook to check the colour is what you want before using it to paint the design. These small colour studies also help with thread selection when it comes to matching shades to your drawings.

Always let paints dry completely before tracing the design onto some water-soluble film. If your design is not completely dry, the water-soluble topping will dissolve and stick to the page, creating a hole in the film when it's pulled away.

The patch base fabric must be sandwiched in

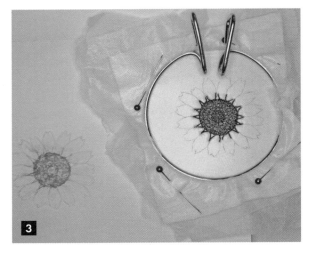

between a layer of tear-away backing, and the water-soluble film with the drawing marked out before framing up in an embroidery hoop for free-motion embroidery **(Fig. 1.)**.

For the centre of the flower, the same circular technique that was used for the snake clutch bag embroidery project was used. Move the fabric around in circular motions, using a chestnut colour thread to create small circles, similar to French knots to replicate the seeds inside a sunflower. Have the machine feed dogs down and all stitch length settings set to zero

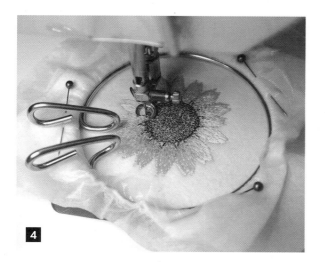

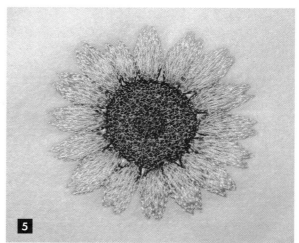

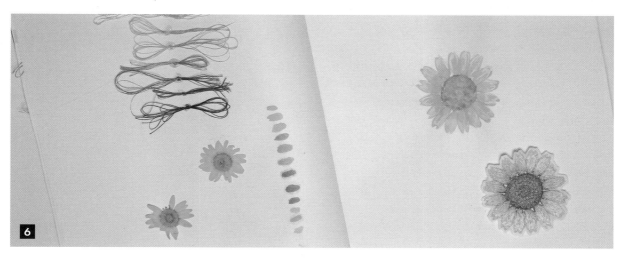

(Fig. 2.). This was topped with a mid-brown thread to outline the small circles, adding an even darker shade in the middle of the circle and around the edges to capture the unique characteristics of the centre of a sunflower (Fig. 3.).

The petals are outlined in the lighter yellow thread choice before using the satin stitch effect for the edges, and filling in with some regular free-motion for shading with a darker yellow to build depth in the petals (Fig. 4.).

When the embroidery is ready to be applied to your chosen garment, remove all the backing and topping materials before cutting out (Fig. 5.).

Cut the patch out no closer than 1.5 millimetres to the edge, so as to not catch any threads and allow enough fabric to stitch onto your garments (Fig. 6.).

Your patch does not have to be the same shape as your design, nor does it have to be close to the embroidery edge. You can cut out a completely different shape to your embroidery if you like, and stitch the patch down with a coloured satin stitch outline as an extra feature.

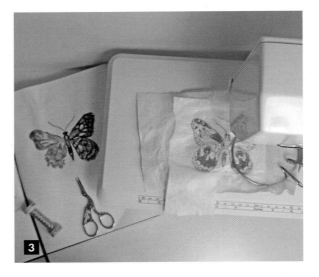

DETAILED PATCH EMBROIDERY

When starting to work on more detailed embroidered patches, it's easy to over stitch into a piece and end up with areas that are far too heavily stitched. Using tear-away backing behind a medium weight, non-fraying fabric, like felt, can make the process easier for beginners. It is important not to end up with dense areas of stitching as they can be tricky to continue stitching back into if you want to add to your design. Try and plan your detail ahead in your drawings! It's not always easy to foresee how a motif or design will end up in embroidery – however, considering your colour choices ahead and where they might be used can be helpful.

In this example a butterfly has been drawn from scratch using paints, fine liners, and coloured pencils to create a colour story and different shapes within the wings, although you can use any medium you wish to come up with your design **(Fig. 1.)**.

Water-soluble film is placed over the drawing to trace out the main elements using any regular ball point pen. To get perfect opposite sides when working with symmetrical or mirrored designs, draw one half onto the film, then flip and draw the other **(Fig. 2.)**.

Always sandwich your patch material – as with other projects – between the clear topping with the design on it and some tear-away backing, and pin in place. This really helps with detailed work.

Your sewing machine should be set to free-motion, with feed dogs down and no stitch length or width. If you are not yet familiar with this technique, see 'Techniques & Tips'. By outlining the design first with either the most neutral colour in your palette, or the

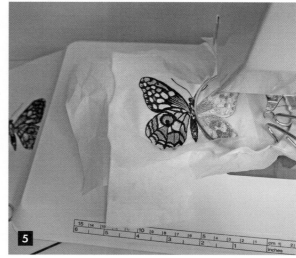

colour you wish to outline the embroidery, you will secure the design into place and avoid any movement when filling in colours. This is less essential for smaller, less detailed embroideries that don't require as much moving around of the hoop. A neutral off-white was used for this butterfly patch, though since black is also a dominant colour in the design, it would also have worked. Next it's time to start adding colour! Move the hoop with both hands to 'paint' colours with stitch using the free-motion technique **(Fig. 3.)**.

TIP: If you're already confident with free-motion, add a bit of stitch width/zig-zag to your machine settings as suggested in previous projects. This will also provide a smooth satin stitch which gives a more luxurious finish **(Fig. 4.)**.

Consider which order to stitch the colours in, which colours need to stand out most and which need to be blended in with other colours. Thinking about the order of colours can really change the effect of the design. For example, the strong black of the butterfly has been embroidered last on this patch for the most impact **(Fig. 5.)**.

These patches can be applied to any garment, either by hand stitching with a needle and thread, or by setting your machine to a zig-zag setting with a straight foot and sewing round the edges of the patch.

Use as a statement piece on its own on a T-shirt, the back pocket of your jeans (on the top to keep the pocket in use) or make enough of them in various designs and sizes to cover a coat or a dress **(Fig. 6.)**.

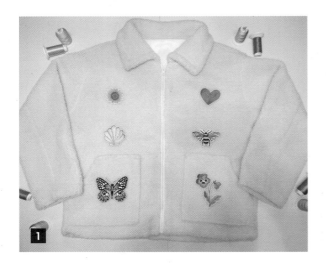

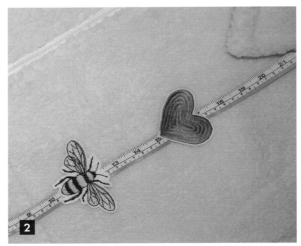

APPLYING YOUR PATCHES TO GARMENTS

The application of fabric onto another piece of fabric is called appliqué. Play around with the placement of patches before deciding on a final composition, considering different placement options and photographing each one to help compare them against one another to decide on your favourite. Try a few different garments if you have options and aren't sure which one to customise **(Fig. 1.)**.

TIP: If you're going for a more structured layout like the one in this project, measure out your placements to make sure the patches all line up perfectly **(Fig. 2.)**. This fluffy jacket was chosen for a playful upcycle project, which consists of six different patches of varying degrees of difficulty.

High pile materials like this jacket is made of can make it more difficult to appliqué onto and cause the patch to move around, so be sure they are secured in multiple points with pins **(Fig. 3.)**. Iron-on fabric fuse, (or Bondaweb) doesn't work well with high pile materials, so it is worth taking the extra time to secure with stitches. When stitching patches down onto fluffy garments (either by hand or machine), it helps to push the pile outwards from under the patch as you stitch around it.

Appliquéing onto lined garments can be tricky as you don't want to sew all the way through to the lining if you want to achieve a premium look. Either make a commitment to take care and spend more time avoiding the lining, or just to stitch all the way through - don't mix them up. If you accidentally catch the lining whilst trying to avoid it, you could risk catching the inner lining fabric in an area that's not directly beneath your patch, causing the garment to pull and pucker **(Fig. 4.)**.

If you decide to sew all the way through the lining, pin

the patches in place, making sure the pins go through every layer. This is the simpler option for beginners.

Alternatively, patches can be sewn down on your machine using a moderate zig-zag width and length. If you wish to avoid catching the lining with machine application, the lining of the garment will need to be opened in order to access the area, and then re-sealed when complete. This is an advanced option and only recommended for those who are confident in closing the garment lining afterwards.

TAKE WORKING ON PATCHES FURTHER

Create one-off motifs for T-shirts, or go crazy and make tens of unique designs and cover a jacket, rucksack or some jeans!

If you're using patches to cover stains or repair holes, remember to consider this when contemplating a composition. Make sure that these elements have been covered completely and, in the cases of holes, that the patch is large enough to conceal it with at least 5 millimetres of fabric remaining around it in order to stitch the patch on neatly.

free-motion direct onto garments

Embroidering directly onto clothes, especially garments made of thinner fabric, is what many people struggle with when they start on more advanced free-motion embroidery techniques. Thinner fabrics can pucker easily and develop holes if not handled correctly, but with patience, free-motion embroidery can be done on any material. Free-motion embroidery direct onto garments does require a lot of practice so if you're not confident, practice your skills on similar fabric first. The trick is to always use an embroidery hoop, make sure your tension on your machine is perfect and use backings to stabilise the main fabric.

simple floral t-shirt

*You will learn: Turning line-drawings into free-motion.
Use free-motion embroidery directly onto garments instead of using patches to
create beautiful, delicate results. With this project you will start with simple line
drawings to learn how to work your designs onto garments.*

Skill Level:
Improving Beginner

You will need
- Tear-Away Backing
- Water-Soluble Film
- Plain Cotton T-shirt
  (pre-owned)

Equipment
- Sewing Machine
  (I use a Bernina1008)
- Embroidery Foot
- Small Embroidery Scissors
- Pen
- Spring Embroidery Hoop

Embroidery threads
- Gunold Sulky 1005
- Gunold Cotty 100
  (used for bobbin thread
  and hand sewing)

Line drawings are the best designs to start with when learning how to free-motion directly onto garments and thinner materials. They are simple, only require one thread colour, and can look beautiful and delicate when completed. Embroidering onto thin cottons with your machine can be daunting at first; it can be easy to get the tension wrong or go over your lines too much, causing puckering or holes in your garment or fabric. Always back your thin fabrics, test the tension on some similar fabric beforehand, and do your best not to over-sew on these types of materials. Starting with simple designs with no shading and fewer colour changes is the best way to begin with garments like T-shirts.

Start by choosing an object to draw to create your line drawing design. Flowers make beautiful line illustrations for embroidery and are easier to draw than something like animals, for example. Your drawings should be quick and effortless - don't worry too much about precision; the rawness is often the beauty of these types of designs.

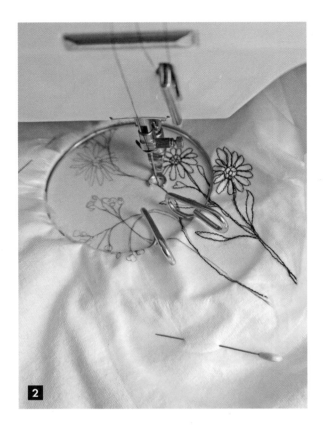

Create as many drawings as you can to give yourself lots of choice **(Fig. 1.)**.

Cover your whole design with a sheet of water-soluble film, leaving a few centimetres all round for stability. Lightly trace out the drawing using any regular pen – this is also an opportunity to slightly change any elements you're not happy with, or miss things out you don't wish to include.

Test the tension of your sewing machine to make sure it will not eat the fabric and then place a piece of tear-away backing fabric inside your garment where you will be stitching the design. Carefully pin the water-soluble film on the top of the garment in the same place. The pins should go through all three layers – topping, garment fabric and backing. Before jumping in and beginning to embroider, hold the piece up to make sure you're happy with

the placement, or even try it on carefully in a mirror, adjusting it slightly if it's not in the right place. It can be easy to pin the design in a crooked position, so just make sure you're happy with where it's located – once the embroidery is complete it can be very difficult to remove, especially with thin fabrics.

Frame up the piece where you wish to begin embroidering. Any embroidery hoop can be used, however a spring hoop is very convenient as it can be undone, adjusted, and moved around the fabric with ease **(Fig. 2.)**.

Make sure the settings on your machine are set to free-motion embroidery – all stitch lengths set to zero and your feed dogs are down. Use your hands to carefully move the hoop around under the needle whilst it's moving up and down to draw out the design (in-depth instructions on free-motion embroidery can

4

be found under 'Free-Motion Sewing' in 'Techniques & Tips'). Try to keep your fingers away from the needle and be especially careful with smaller hoops as the smaller diameter means your hands are closer to the needle.

When embroidering line drawings, you will need to go over each line at least twice to make sure that the stitches are secure – just a single line is likely to come undone when caught accidentally, or washed **(Fig. 3.)**.

Once the entire design is complete and all your lines have been embroidered, un-hoop the project and remove all tear-away backing and topping. Both should come away quite easily. It can also be a good way of testing how secure your stitches are. If the two come away without pulling the stitches, then they should be durable enough to withstand machine

washing **(Fig. 4.)**. Any small bits of water-soluble film trapped inside detailed elements will come away with a steam or a wash.

TIPS FOR FREE-MOTIONING DIRECTLY ONTO LIGHTWEIGHT MATERIALS

If you're nervous about embroidering onto a lightweight garment like a cotton T-shirt, find some scrap fabric of similar density and practise free-motioning with this first, with the backing in place. Simple line free-motion embroidery looks great when you use long, free movements for longer stitches, as opposed to lots of tiny ones bunched together. This is more difficult so, if you are a beginner, start slowly and only move the hoop as quickly as you are comfortable with!

floral blouse

You will learn: Simple line embroidery on tricky garments.
Using the same embroidered line drawing technique as the previous floral T-shirt,
this project introduces you to working with fabrics that are more difficult to work
with. Thin fabrics are prone to puckering and it's harder to unpick mistakes.

Skill Level:
Improving Beginner

You will need
- Tear-Away Backing
- Water-Soluble Film
- Plain Poplin Shirt
  (pre-owned))

Equipment
- Sewing Machine
  (I use a Bernina 1008)
- Embroidery Foot
- Small Embroidery Scissors
- Pen
- Spring Embroidery Hoop

Embroidery threads
- Gunold Sulky 1005
- Gunold Cotty 100
  (used for bobbin thread
  and hand sewing)

Plain poplin shirts make great garments for free-motion line embroidery designs. The smooth, thin fabric makes the stitches stand out and appear raised. If you don't have a shirt in your wardrobe, there's a good chance you might find one on your local charity shop!

The same line drawing techniques were used for the illustrations on this shirt on the previous project. Studying a selection of flowers, six A5 sized pieces of plain white paper were drawn on free-hand using a black pen **(Fig. 1.)**.

By placing the drawings in different arrangements around the shirt, three final pieces were selected for the final design **(Fig. 2.)**. Get creative by drawing different arrangements and bunches of flowers to make unique compositions.

Using a pen, trace your chosen drawings onto a small sheet of water-soluble film, and pin it on your garment with the tear-away backing stabiliser underneath **(Fig. 3.)**.

Embroidering on a poplin shirt is easier than on a cotton T-shirt because poplin isn't a stretchy fabric. However, pins and needles can often leave marks in delicate poplin, so be careful how long you leave them in when securing the base and top fabrics, and

try to avoid unpicking any stitches in case these leave holes.

For the embroidery on the sleeve, a part of one of the illustrations was used to create a smaller, less heavily decorated design on the arm.

Embroidering onto the main body is relatively easy, especially if your shirt has buttons as you can open it up for easier access and a flatter surface. What makes this project more difficult than the previous project is the embroidery on the sleeves. The table attachment on your sewing machine, which helps a lot with free-motion embroidery, will need to be removed to fit the sleeve over **(Fig. 4.)**. Doing this will mean that during the stitch process, the hoop

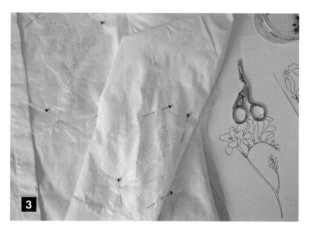

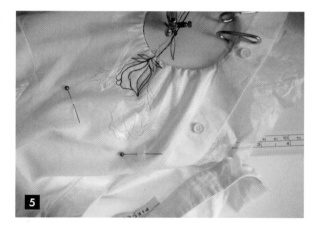

is likely to rock back and forth on the machine arm, which can affect the tidiness of the embroidery. If you're not confident in free-motioning without the assistance of the table to keep your hoop stable and flat, do some practice runs without it until you're satisfied with the result, or avoid embroidering on the sleeve completely! **(Fig. 5.)**.

LINE-DRAWING EMBROIDERY TIPS

Using the same colour for your bobbin thread as you use for you top thread can be useful for designs that only use one colour. It will help to stop small flecks of under thread from peeking through to the top. It also makes it easier to set your tension, as you can focus

solely on the stability without having to worry about keeping the white thread from coming through to the top of the embroidery.

Draw from a range of different subjects for a unique look. Draw your pets or create hand-written messages and combine them all together for something that is completely personal to you.

Consider what colours look best on the colour of your shirt. Go for dramatic contrast - white and black always contrast well; neon colours look good on pastels; and colours from the opposite sides of the colour wheel stand out. Alternatively, you can go subtle – different shades of the same colour can create a beautiful, embossed effect.

pink 'peachy' midi skirt

*You will learn: Creating a simple repeat pattern on an existing garment.
Be inspired by this project and transform plain garments into beautiful, patterned
pieces. Your designs don't need to be big or detailed to elevate a piece. With
design, sometimes small and simple can be just as impactful as large and bold.*

Skill Level:
Beginner

You will need
- Tear-Away Backing
- Vintage Linen Pink Skirt
  (charity shop buy)

Equipment
- Sewing Machine
  (I use a Bernina 1008)
- Pins
- Embroidery Foot
- Small Embroidery Scissors
- Spring Embroidery Hoop

Embroidery threads
- Gunold Sulky 1168
- Gunold Sulky 1272
- Gunold Cotty 1317
- Gunold Cotty 100
  (used for bobbin thread)

Charity shops are fantastic places to find unique pieces like this handmade pink linen skirt. You can create any pattern you like with free-motion embroidery. Use it to add decoration and interest to plain garments, or mix with patterned fabrics for more detail. Be as structured or as random as you like with design placement although if you're using something that already has a pattern like spots or stripes, this may dictate where you add your embroidery.

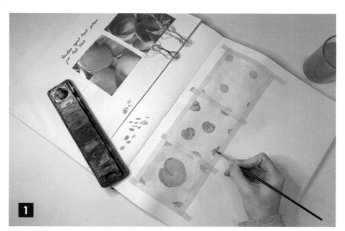

The motifs you design can be as large or small, or as close together or far apart as you like. The peaches for this skirt were painted in water colour with small details added using coloured pencils in a random formation. Draw a small section of how you wish your finished repeat to look. This will really help you decide on your final placement and the sizes of your designs. For this design, I chose small designs, irregularly scattered. You may want to create multiple pages with different pattern ideas before choosing which works best as a larger repeat **(Fig. 1.).**

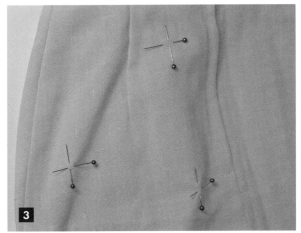

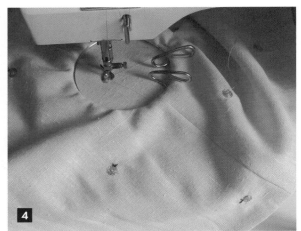

Some washi tape was used to create borders between different design options, and pulled away when the three compositions had been finished **(Fig. 2.)**.

Create a few small thread stories by your design to help choose which shades will look best on your garment. Once your design is finalised and you've made your thread choices, mark out the placements for your repeat pattern with some pins. The pins have been marked out randomly on this pink linen skirt, with similar distances between each one for a looser, less structured look. This is the easiest way to create a repeat embroidery pattern, however you can

challenge yourself with a more structured, planned composition. You can use small stickers or an air-erasable pen instead of pins if your fabric is prone to leaving pin marks **(Fig. 3.)**.

The ditsy peach pattern embroidered onto this pink skirt is quite spaced out, so small pieces of backing were used for each motif. No water-soluble film was used as the peaches were very small and simple to stitch and didn't require any guidelines.

Going completely free-hand is a great way to create embroidered patterns that look more care-free and natural, showing the beauty of each motif not

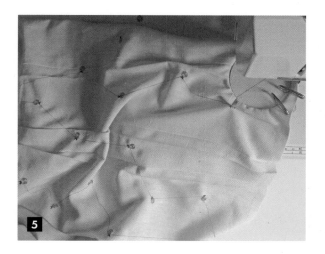

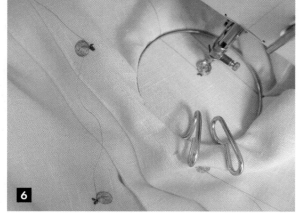

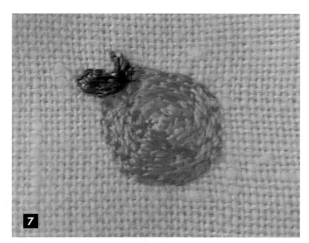

looking exactly the same **(Fig. 4.)**. If your design is more detailed, tracing out the motifs onto some water-soluble film and using this as a guide will obtain the best results, also acting as an extra stabiliser for very thin materials.

Try to plan which order you will stitch your colours in. It will really help reduce the amount of time you spend threading the changing colours! After each colour has been completed, be sure to cut away any jump stitches – especially long ones – before moving onto the next colour **(Fig. 5.)**. Stitches can pull the garment between motifs, making it tricky to frame up the fabric in a hoop. The lightest colour was used first on this peach repeat design, before moving onto the small green leaf detail and then finishing off the characteristic peach details with a darker coral colour **(Fig. 6.)**.

Remember to carefully remove any backing or topping used for the stitching process once the piece is complete **(Fig. 7.)**.

CREATING PATTERNS WITH EMBROIDERY

For a more structured repeat pattern, use marked out dressmaker's pattern paper or grid paper to help place your pins or, alternatively, measure it out with a tape measure. If you're working onto an already patterned garment then you may not need to do this. The possibilities are endless. Miniature hearts or spots are simple motifs that will lift a plain garment and look cute both randomly placed or in a more structured design. Take two different colour garments and make them a matching set by embroidering a simple shape all over each piece in the colour of the coordinating garment. This technique can be used to patch up multiple holes in old garments by placing small scraps of fabric (similar in colour to the base) on the inside of the garment where the holes are, and embroidering over them.

'be kind' blouse

You will learn: Using patterned garments to guide free-motion.
Embroidery can be used to amplify garments that are already colourful and patterned. Take this top as an example! Using the floral design as a base to work on, changing colours and incorporating lettering creates a statement piece.

Skill Level:
Intermediate

You will need
- Tear-Away Backing
- Water-Soluble Film
- Patterned Blouse
  (charity shop buy)

Equipment
- Sewing Machine
  (I use a Bernina 1008)
- Straight Foot
- Embroidery Foot
- Small Embroidery Scissors
- Small Embroidery Hoop

Embroidery threads
- Gunold Poly 40
  (neon pink)
- Gunold Sulky 1001
- Gunold Sulky 1067
- Gunold Sulky 1023
- Gunold Sulky 1019

Slogans and phrases are a great way to personalise and upcycle your existing wardrobe! There's a wealth of positive quotes out there, with something that speaks to everyone. It's easy to think that slogans look best as stand-out statements on plain items, but this project shows how you can update an old, patterned top with some upbeat wording just as effectively.

Start by tracing out the text in your chosen size and font onto some water-soluble film **(Fig. 1.)**. Using water-soluble film allows you to see the outline of where you will be stitching and also provides more structure to thinner fabrics. Design your own handwritten or bubble font, or simply print out the wording from a computer and trace it.

Pin your chosen text to your garment in the desired position. Add some embroidery stabiliser or tear-away backing underneath the patterned fabric, so that the floral material is sandwiched in-between the film and backing materials. These two additional materials are what helps to avoid puckering on lightweight fabrics, especially when using heavy embroidery. The more stabiliser used, the less puckering will occur so if you add another under-layer, this can help.

At this stage, depending on the style of lettering chosen and your personal preferences, the outline of the text can be sewn using either a straight stitch with a regular foot, or you can change to free-motion settings and outline the text with the garment and stabiliser materials framed in a hoop for tension. All technique options can be found in 'Techniques & Tips'.

Think about which flowers or elements of the pattern you want to be hidden by the text, and which you'd like to poke out over the lettering **(Fig. 2.)**.

It's important to outline all the text before filling in with free-motion embroidery to keep all the materials secure together. If each letter is outlined and filled in before moving onto the next, the film with the design can move and the position of the remaining text might not be as intended.

Step back and have a look at your embroidered piece before removing all the stabilisers. If the text appears too hidden at this stage, add more embroidery to the lettering to hide some of the patterned elements concealing parts of the letters that make them difficult to read— it is your decision how legible you want your lettering to be. In this project, a few sections were filled in to make the quote easier to read and the text was outlined twice with a straight stitch **(Fig. 3.)**.

You can leave the design simple and remove the backing and topping materials or keep the stabiliser materials attached and continue embroidering, stitching over the flowers to add texture as done in this example **(Fig. 4.)**. Use colours matching the motifs in the pattern, or completely change it up by stitching over them with new colours you wish to add to the design **(Fig. 5.)**.

When altering the colours of the flowers with free-motion embroidery, you can use basic free-motion or satin stitch effect free-motion (see both 'Free-Motion Sewing' and 'Satin Stitch Free-Motion' in 'Techniques & Tips') depending on your ability. Regular free-motion, using the back and forth motion of your hands to move the hoop is much easier than satin stitching.

USE PATTERNS TO YOUR ADVANTAGE

Miss out the text in this project if you wish, and just use the pattern as a guide for your free-motion embroidery skills to add detail to the existing design by changing colours, or adding small motifs in between the florals, like bees, butterflies or hidden animals!

Busy patterns can tend to hide the embroidered lettering – bright, contrasting threads like the neon pink used in this project will stand out best from the original fabric design. If you're using text with patterned garments, consider whether you'd like it to blend in or stand out when making your thread choices.

cutwork denim top

You will learn: Combining free-motion embroidery with cutwork.
In this project we will look at combining cutwork denim with embroidery to create delicate results similar to broderie anglaise. Denim is very forgiving and is a fantastic material to pair with embroidery due to its durability.

Skill Level:
Intermediate

You will need
- Tear-Away Backing
- Water-Soluble Film
- Net/Tulle
- Denim Top
  (pre-owned)

Equipment
- Sewing Machine
  (I use a Bernina 1008)
- Embroidery Foot
- Small Embroidery Scissors
- Spring Embroidery Hoop

Embroidery threads
- Gunold Sulky 1001
- Gunold Cotty 100
  (used for bobbin thread)

Denim is a very forgiving fabric. It's quite dense and doesn't have much stretch to it, so it is less likely to pucker making it perfect for heavy stitching. If you are planning a lot of embroidery on your piece, it is also not essential to use backing. Additionally, topping materials only need to act as design guides rather than for stabilisation.

Cutwork with embroidery also works well on denim because of its structure and robustness. Small holes tend to hold their shape and bigger holes can be held in place with some thin, sheer fabric, as shown in this project.

The intricate border pattern was designed using a Portuguese tile for inspiration – a great example of how you can use household objects, trinkets and keepsakes for inspiration and as drawing subjects **(Fig. 1.)**. The width of the top was measured and a to-size template made on a piece of paper. You only need to draw your cutwork design on half the top if the design is a mirror image of itself. When working with symmetrical or mirrored designs, cut a piece of water-soluble film twice as long as your drawing and trace

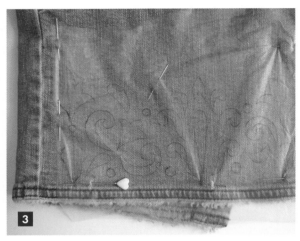

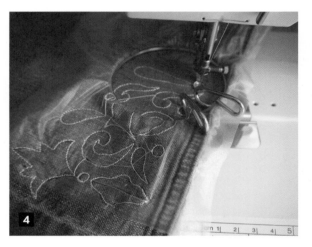

out the first half, leaving plenty of room for the other half before flipping it face side down (so that the side you've just drawn your design into is against the page), and continue to draw the other half, meeting the design in the middle (Fig. 2.). This will ensure that the embroidery is identical on either side. This method of achieving mirrored and symmetrical designs easily, without measuring the other side to be identical, also works for drawings like butterflies and bees.

Pin the water-soluble film in place across the border of the denim top without any tear-away backing behind – this would mean extra work when

removing all the small shapes of backing before performing the cutwork – so unless the material needs stabilisation, it saves time not using backing in this instance (Fig. 3.).

With the marked-out film pinned to the garment, hoop up the piece at one end and begin to free-motion around the shapes individually, lifting the foot in between each one. Slow movements of the hand work best for cutwork, as the stitches will act as a barrier for any fraying edges and need to be secure. No need for a back-and-forth motion for simple lines, these can be stitched over two or three times

consecutively for an even density all the way around **(Fig. 4.)**. This is the border of the cutwork and will keep the raw edges from fraying too much. Plain white thread was used on this denim top for a fresh, clean look, although you can match the base fabric colour so that it blends in, or even make a feature out of the lines and use a shade that stands out against the garment!

Once all the shapes in the design have been outlined, the water-soluble film that acted as a design guide can be removed, along with any backing fabrics if they were needed. Make sure that all stabiliser materials have been removed at this stage, including any small shapes, otherwise they may peek through the gaps and be seen from the front **(Fig. 5.)**.

At this stage, you could leave the piece as it is, with a simple yet beautiful line embroidered border feature. However, if you are continuing with the cutwork effect, check over all the lines to make sure

there are no loose elements which could allow the fraying to 'bleed' outside the embroidered shapes. If all is secure, it's safe to begin cutting the shapes out from inside the stitch lines (be sure not to cut around the shapes!). If there are any frayed bits, sew back over any loose areas until they are secure before beginning any cutwork. Try not to cut too close to the lines as this will remove yarns that the embroidery is holding onto, and risks cutting through the threads themselves, two millimetres is close enough for the desired effect **(Fig. 6.)**.

Depending on your rdesign and the fabric your garment is made up of, you could finish the project here, or you may need to add some sheer material to the back of the design. Some of the cutwork shapes that make up the main features of this design are quite large and needed a bit of stability **(Fig. 7.)**. Some plain netting was placed on the inside of the garment, and sewn in place, embroidering around

7

all the shapes just once more to secure the fabric, before cutting away any excess from the back of the piece. When embroidering just one line of stitch, it's important to do a miniature 'backtack', by going back over a few stitches at the beginning and at the end of the stitch line to avoid it from coming loose.

The back of this denim blouse already had an open feature with buttons to close the top at the nape of the neck. This detail was used as part of the design with the cutwork border continued around to the back of the top and up the central seams, meeting the buttons at the top for a statement open back design

(Fig. 8.).

To give the opposite effect to cutwork, you can use this technique for some contrasting appliqué designs. Layer another piece of denim or any material of your choice on top of the garment and embroider the design onto both pieces together **(Fig. 9.) (Fig. 10.)**. When complete, cut away the top fabric approximately two millimetres away from the outer sides of the shapes to reveal the main base underneath. Using two different shades of denim has given a beautiful, embossed effect **(Fig. 11.)**.

CUTWORK EMBROIDERY TIPS

Larger cutwork designs work best on thick materials like the denim top used in this project, but don't let that stop you experimenting with other fabrics. Generally, the thinner the piece, the smaller the holes should be to avoid them losing their shape. However, this can be fixed by adding sheer fabrics like the net in this project.

You can stitch any fabric behind cutwork for a reverse appliqué effect too. Use plain block colour or patterned fabric scraps, or even embroider your own fabric design that can be revealed by the open shapes.

For a high-end effect, and to hide raw edges if you don't like this look, slowly go around the edges with a very tight zig-zag stitch with either a straight foot or an embroidery foot depending on the nature of your design. This will conceal the natural edges and give a traditional broderie anglaise look too!

daisy cardigan

You will learn: Decorating buttons with embroidery.
This project introduces the idea of embroidering buttons to decorate a garment. If you have an old cardigan with dated buttons at the back of your wardrobe, this is a great way to make it look like a designer item!

Skill Level:
Intermediate

You will need
- Iron on Adhesive/ Bondaweb
- Water-Soluble Film
- Lilac Cotton
- Orange/Gold Seed Beads
- Fleece for padding
- Knitted Lilac Cardigan (pre-owned)

Equipment
- Drawing Compass
- Sewing Machine (I use a Bernina 1008)
- Embroidery Foot
- Small Embroidery Scissors
- Spring Embroidery Hoop
- Beading Needle
- Hand Sewing Needle

Embroidery threads
- Gunold Sulky 1001
- Gunold Sulky 0508
- Gunold Sulky 1025
- Gunold Cotty 100 (used for bobbin thread)

1

Firstly, choose some scrap fabric to match the colour of the cardigan, making sure there's enough to cover all the buttons before starting. This doesn't have to be the same colour as your cardigan, the fabric can be a completely different colour. If you plan on covering the entire button with embroidery and embellishment then the base colour really doesn't matter.

Before starting with your design, it's important to measure your button. Measuring the radius of the button and setting a compass to this width, draw out a circle the same size to create your design area. If you're lucky enough to have a spare button for your cardigan, simply draw around it. Double your radius and create another, larger circle surrounding the first one – this will be the area of fabric you will cut out. Once both circles are marked out (the smaller one inside the larger) you can start to design your new buttons. **(Fig. 1.)**.

Pressed daisies and dried flowers were used as drawing subjects for the buttons. Two colour-ways were created with basic colouring pencils as a drawing medium **(Fig. 2.)**. Hold some threads against your material to help direct the colour choices of your drawings. I like to draw my designs in full colour because I find if I start to embroider my design without proper decision making, I can be unhappy with my design or the amount of colour contrast in my design **(Fig. 3.)**.

Using a pen, transfer your drawing onto a sheet of water-soluble film. Mark out the design as well as

the larger outer circle, leaving out the inner circle that indicated the size of the button - unless you wish to add this as a stitched feature **(Fig. 4.)**. Back your chosen fabric with some iron-on adhesive (enough for all your buttons plus the extra space around them) for stability and to help reduce fraying edges – this will not be removed at the end which is why it should be stuck down securely **(Fig. 5.)**.

The water-soluble film should be pinned in place as flat as possible on top of the fabric, making sure that the iron-on adhesive underneath covers the entire design area including the circular border **(Fig. 6.)**. The

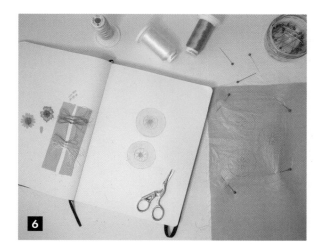

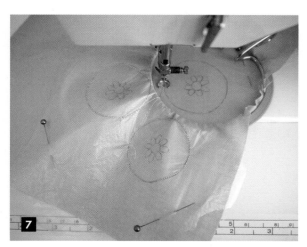

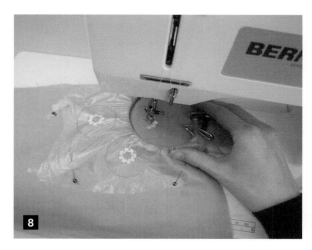

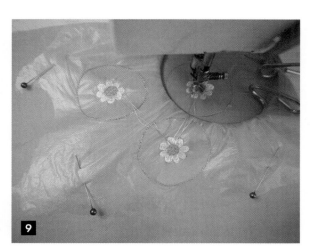

first thread shade stitched should be the one closest in colour to the base fabric and should be used to trace the outer circle two or three times. Circles are very difficult to get perfect with free-motion - the backing will help but make sure that when hooped up the circle is completely symmetrical and hasn't warped. Try to stitch around the entire circle without moving the hoop to a new section of the fabric **(Fig. 7.)**.

Once the circles have been stitched, proceed with the design embroidery. For this lilac cardigan, the white and yellow daisies were embroidered using the zig-zag free-motion technique found in 'Satin Stitch

Free-Motion' in 'Techniques & Tips', for a beautiful satin effect on the white petal edges. The inside of the petals were filled in with an ivory colour using regular free-motion to create shading. Small differences in colour creates nice, subtle detail **(Fig. 8.)**.

For the centre of the daisies, free-motion was used in small, circular motions to create miniature rounds with a golden yellow embroidery thread. This was done in preparation for beading but can be left as a unique feature of its own **(Fig. 9.)**.

Once all the embroidery is complete and before adding any hand touches, remove the water-soluble topping

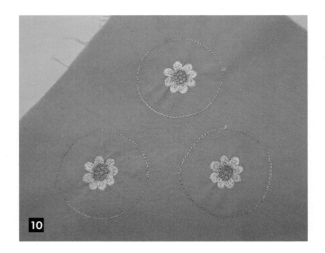

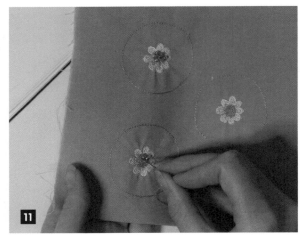

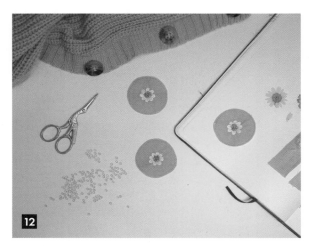

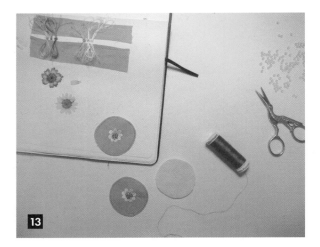

and press the piece once again with a hot iron to make sure the backing is still secure. Allow to cool completely before doing any more work on these to ensure the backing fuses correctly **(Fig. 10.)**.

Tiny, delicate golden orange seed beads were hand beaded to fill in the small circular holes left by the yellow embroidery. When using hand finishes like beading, do not use Sulky embroidery threads as these are prone to fraying and breaking. Use a regular cotton thread in a similar colour to your base fabric or to match your beads. Double knot your thread and then, starting from the back, create a few

small stitches to secure the thread, before proceeding to hand bead. Finish off at the back of the design to secure the thread before trimming any threads **(Fig. 11.)**. If you're beading, do this before cutting the circle shapes out; it helps to have extra fabric to hold when beading and prevents the edges from fraying while you work with them **(Fig. 12.)**.

Using padding on the button is optional, but when decorating buttons with hard edges, ridges and a dip in the centre, adding some thickness can help to smooth the surface out for a better quality finish. The colour of your padding fabric doesn't matter – as

long as it cannot be seen through the front of the piece. Using your circular designs as a template, cut circles out of your chosen padding fabric. Fleece is fantastic as padding, as it's soft and spongy but felt can also work although it can sometimes be a little bit too rigid **(Fig. 13.)**.

Place the padding under your embroidered design and make a small running stitch all the way around the edge of the circle to bind them together. Make sure the stitches of the running stitch are quite short in length and are inside the embroidered line you stitched earlier. Do this all the way around the shape just once, and pull the thread so that the edges start to gather in **(Fig. 14.)**.

Place the piece of fabric over the button and hold the embroidery design central with one hand, pulling the thread as tight as possible without it snapping so that the edges gather and tighten around the button. If the circular piece was cut at the right size, it should come together nicely underneath the button. Keep your needle threaded so you can then secure the button cover with a few stitches.**(Fig. 15.)**.

The new button will need to be secure. Stitch all the way through the stitches that held the original button in place from one side to the other as many times as you feel necessary, and all the way through to the inside of the cardigan. These will be used a lot to open and close the cardigan so they must not be loose! This part can be fiddly and tough, so if you're not used to sewing through lots of layers then using a thimble could help.

Decorating buttons doesn't have to be restricted to cardigans – try this on coats with buttons too for some statement outerwear. Anything that closes with button fastenings can be upcycled in this way - jeans, jackets, shirts and skirts. Just make sure you sew them on securely enough to be buttoned and unbuttoned constantly.

MORE IDEAS FOR DECORATING BUTTONS

Make your buttons a different colour to your knitwear, or go for a colourful look and make them all different colours and designs. I love the idea of flowers, hearts, rainbows and animals all on one cardigan - what a very unique jumper that would be!

Consider using sheer fabrics if you want to make a feature out of the padding, trap beads or charms between them or even have the original button slightly visible underneath.

celestial crop top

You will learn: Embroidering on satin with a hint of beading.
Embroidery and bead work is a match made in heaven! Here we look at beading
and embroidering onto lightweight materials with metallic threads which can be
difficult to work with and need special care.

Skill Level:
Advanced

You will need
- Tear-Away Backing
- Water-Soluble Film
- Premium Crystal Beads in Dark Emerald Green
- Black Satin Crop Top (pre owned)

Equipment
- Sewing Machine (I use a Bernina 1008)
- Embroidery Foot
- Small Embroidery Scissors
- Spring Embroidery Hoop
- Beading Needle

Embroidery threads
- Gunold Mety 7/2 7001
- Madeira 1660
- Gunold Cotty 100 (used for bobbin thread)
- Gunold Cotty 300 (hand beading thread)

Although crop tops aren't in everyone's wardrobe, they provide the perfect base for statement party wear. This project will not only inspire turning those basic bralettes into a work of art for your body, but also teach you how to embroider onto slippery fabrics like satin and silk that can be tricky to work with.

This plain black satin V-neck bralette was decorated with metallic celestial embroidery using some sparkly hair accessories for inspiration. Using your accessories, and items you wish to wear your new customised clothing with as inspiration is a great way to generate imagery – use them as drawing subjects, or even for colour inspiration.

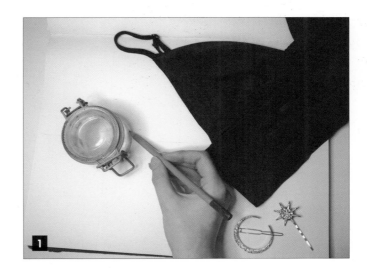

Because the imagery for this design is very symmetrical and consists of circles, a round object was used to draw around before adding some guidelines for the rest of the celestial drawing **(Fig. 1.)**.

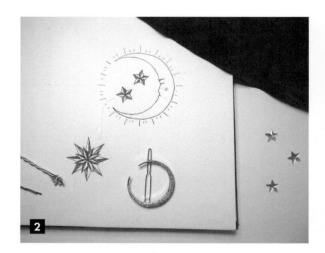

When drawing out your design, don't worry if you make a section you're not happy with. Just re-draw onto some tracing paper and change the elements or make a small sketch of the new element. You can easily replace the section you're not happy with when tracing onto your water-soluble film **(Fig. 2.)**.

For dark coloured fabrics, using a white pen instead of a black one will make the guidelines you draw on the topping much easier to follow. It's worth investing in one if you plan on working on a lot of dark garments and materials **(Fig. 3.)**.

Pin the water-soluble film on the garment with some tear-away backing behind the fabric. Using these materials will help you to work with embroidery on silky fabrics that have lots of movement; they stabilise the main body whilst you embroider and help to reduce puckering which can be difficult to avoid on fragile garments **(Fig. 4.)**.

Since the crop top was already made in a luscious shiny fabric, a mixture of metallic and mink-coloured threads were chosen to further add to the existing opulence for even more shine and impact **(Fig. 5.)**. This is after all, a garment best suited for parties, so why not enhance that even more?

Metallics can be problematic threads to embroider with, so if you're new to free-motion embroidery, then stick to regular Sulky threads until you're confident in your skills. Metallic threads often require different tensions to usual embroidery threads, and can snap often (not great for those who are more impatient). Make some small tests on scrap fabrics similar to your garment first, and just be extra careful when stitching with these types of threads. Use a slow to moderate needle speed when free-motioning by not pressing down too hard on the embroidery machine pedal, and avoid making any quick movements when gliding

the fabric around in the hoop with your hands. Stitches need to be at least 1 millimetre long for the metallic thread to show its shine so slower is definitely better for this! If you notice the metallic thread fraying whilst sewing, cut it away, trim the end, re-thread and go back over your work (these will be noticeable as they will be white) **(Fig. 6.)**.

Stitch direction can affect the overall look of the embroidery and can provide a different texture to your work without changing thread colours. Consider using this to your advantage by focusing on using different stitch directions for blocks of embroidery

next to each other, and see how it can create a subtle contrast with just one colour.

Cut away any jump stitches when the embroidery is complete, and remove all stabiliser materials used during the stitch process **(Fig. 7.)**. Be very careful when removing topping material like water-soluble film from fabrics like the satin on this top, and other delicate fabrics like silk. If you catch a small section of the yarn in the weave it can create an unsightly pull in the garment.

Don't worry too much if the back of your embroidery isn't incredibly neat. However, if it's messy with lots of bunches of threads knotted at the back, it may be an indication that your tension is off **(Fig. 8.)**.

Beading is a beautiful way to elevate your embroidery, and goes beautifully with metallic threads as well as classic embroidery threads. Choose the colours that best complement your embroidery – beads come in all shapes and sizes so there are plenty to choose from and there will no doubt be something to work with any design. Small, metallic jade bicone crystals were chosen for this particular piece, and were dotted around the embroideries on both sides of the top to uplift and add detail to small sections. Using a doubled over piece of thread with your beading needle and knotting it together at the end before making a few initial stitches will help ensure that the beads are nice and secure. You can

make your beaded areas as dense or as sparse as you like depending on your own preference, or dot them around to highlight small areas **(Fig. 9.)**.

EMBROIDERING ON LUXURIOUS FABRICS

Luxurious fabrics can be difficult to embroider on, but as long as they're handled with proper care, they can create quite an impact! Always back delicate fabrics when using free-motion on them, otherwise they will without a doubt pucker - not such a luxurious finish - and in the worst cases, holes can form. Once you've got the knack of working with materials like this you will be able to customise anything from lingerie to knitwear and maybe even tulle!

Other luxurious fabrics include velvet and faux fur. These can also be tricky to embroider onto because of their density and high pile. The trick with these types of materials is to use water-soluble film topping, even if you don't wish to use it to draw out your design and would rather freestyle. It will hold down the pile, making the embroidery stand out more, and in cases of very high pile fabrics like faux fur, keep it from getting tangled in your sewing machine needle.

designing a denim jacket

This final chapter will walk you all the way through designing an upcycled vintage denim jacket, using a mixture of patch embroideries and stitching directly onto the garment. You'll learn everything about the design process from initial idea stages, through drawing and composition concepts, to embroidering - just like a designer would do. Detailed drawings are made to guide the design process and make colour selection, composition and placement of design straight forward. Heavily embroidered garments work out better when planned in advance. You will end up with the best results!

embroidered denim jacket

You will learn: Using multiple techniques to create a beautiful upcycled jacket. Here you'll combine all the techniques in the book to create one big final piece. You'll use embroidered patches, sew straight onto the garment, use straight foot and free-motion foot sewing, and regular free-motion and satin-stitch free-motion.

Skill Level:
Advanced

You will need
- Tear-Away Backing
- Water-Soluble Film
- Black Felt Patch Material
- Levi's Denim Jacket (vintage)

Equipment
- Sewing Machine (I use a Bernina 1008)
- Embroidery Foot
- Straight Foot
- Small Embroidery Scissors
- White POSCA Pen
- Pen
- Spring Embroidery Hoop
- Hand Sewing Needle
- Thimble (optional)

Embroidery threads
- Gunold Cotty 300 (for hand sewn elements)
- Gunold Cotty 100 (used for bobbin thread and hand sewing)

Vintage and second hand denim jackets are everywhere! If you don't already own one yourself, you can find one easily in charity shops, thrift shops, markets and websites that specialise in the sale of pre-loved goods like eBay and Depop. Statement denim jackets are a fashion must, and are often the first thing we think of when considering upcycling clothing with embroidery, because they are so accessible and versatile. Denim is a very easy material to work with – it's durable, non-stretchy and thick, and so holds stitches very well without puckering or breaking. Denim is excellent for embroidery – you can even achieve great results when free-motion embroidering onto them without any backing or topping materials.

DRAWINGS AND ILLUSTRATIONS
Start by deciding on a theme for your embroidery, and make a decision on how heavy and intricate or light and simple you want your finished design to be. If you are not one for big statements, you might just want to add a few delicate details or you might want to completely transform your denim jacket into a brand new, extravagant piece with lots of colour and intricate designs, that make it look like a designer piece worth thousands of pounds.

Flowers Gunold Sulky 1001, 1177, 1049, 1051, 1077, 1222, 1561, 1067, 1023, 1024, 1168, 1019, 1020, 1303, 1263, 1005

Butterflies Gunold Sulky 1001, 1007, 1222, 1029, 1067, 1023, 1024, 1168, 1317, 1263, 1005

Leopard & Tiger Gunold Sulky 1001, 167, 1025, 1168, 1078, 1170, 1130, 1005, 1115, 1020, 1049

Your embroidery design can take inspiration from whatever you like - from wildlife to outer space, underwater scenes or floral designs. The more unique and original your ideas, the better, because no one else will have a similar jacket. I was inspired by butterflies and flowers for this project because they're both very colourful elements of nature which lend themselves well to a vibrant design.

For intricate, detailed embroideries like the ones in this project, your drawings are incredibly important. Drawing in colour is not essential, but it really does help when designing and planning out your compositions to visualise how the finished piece will look. However being spontaneous and going with the flow can create beautiful embroidery results if you would prefer to be more fluid in your design process.

Butterflies make impactful embroideries, although they can be difficult to get right because of their symmetry. The butterfly drawings for this jacket were made using lots of guidelines to help get it right. A ruler was used to mark out the central line and to create parallel lines to mark to curves of the wings. In addition horizontal lines were drawn to make sure that the wings stopped at the same upper and lower

points. The shape was marked out lightly with a pencil, (which involved a lot of erasing and correcting for something of this detail) before being filled in and shaded with coloured pencils and a black fine liner pen **(Fig. 1.)**.

This requires a lot of patience and you can end up taking just as long to generate the imagery as working on the embroidery itself. However, it is worth the time and effort when you get a beautifully symmetrical embroidered butterfly as the end result.

Alternatively, you may wish to create a completely freehand butterfly design (maybe with two different patterned wings). This can be just as charming. Your own vision and drawing style should not be compromised in order to create something perfectly symmetrical, so if you prefer a looser, freer effect just draw freehand and embroider your design accordingly.

Three completely different shaped and patterned butterflies were drawn for this denim jacket project. The intention was to mirror the smaller butterflies on either side of the jacket front pockets, and use the other two, larger, brighter ones for the statement sleeve and back pieces **(Fig. 2.)**.

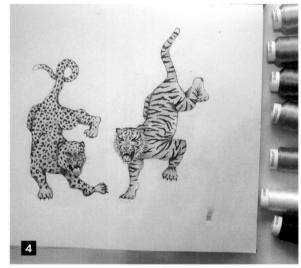

When the butterfly drawings were complete, the floral elements for the jacket were drawn. The designs were made keeping in mind the colours used for the butterfly illustrations and included designs to tie the pieces together. Flowers are quite easy subjects to draw and embroider – they have less symmetry or structure, they are much freer - no petal is the exact same shape and size, so if you make a wrong mark with a pen or stitch, you can just add it to the design as if it were meant to be! Use real flowers from your vase or garden to draw from, or find imagery online or in books. These flowers were inspired by a combination of photos in a copy of Phaidons's Flower Colour Guide by Darroch and Michael Putnam **(Fig. 3.)**.

Just three different flower illustrations were drawn for this project to use for all the embroideries. The intention was to use them on both the front and back of the jacket in various colours and in different scales to stretch the imagery without having to make lots of drawings. These drawings were both mirrored and combined in various compositions to create the illusion of different bunches of flowers all over the jacket. If you're drawing from florals, don't worry

too much about copying their original colours – in fact, they will be even more original if you change the colours to fit with your vision. Only stick to the correct colours if you struggle to create your own colour stories and palettes.

Big cats like tigers and cheetahs look amazing as embroideries, whether you have the skills to embroider them to look realistic, or create them in your own style. The characteristic pattern of their fur contrasts with colourful flowers to create a magnificent design. The big cats were also drawn with coloured pencils and a black pen, using multiple photographs for inspiration and to achieve the desired effect of the two animals looking as though they are circling one another **(Fig. 4.)**.

DESIGNING THE COMPOSITION
With all the illustrations complete, the final design process is coming up with the composition. You may already have in mind how you wish to decorate your garment, but drawing a mock-up of your jacket beforehand will help determine if what you have

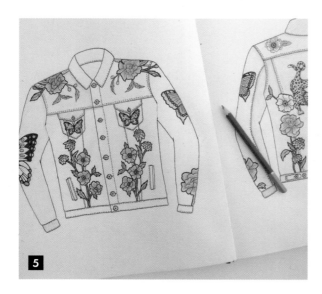

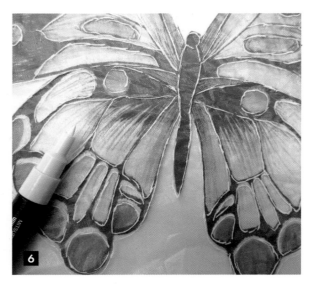

imagined, will work in practice, without making the commitment of stitching everything immediately. If it's a big project that requires a lot of time, the last thing you want is to make mistakes, or wish you had placed one of the embroideries somewhere else.

Draw the garment as in proportion as possible, before creating miniature interpretations of the illustrations on the piece in the desired locations. Doing this in full colour will help to plan out the whole design, and foresee how it will turn out. It could take a few sketches like this to come up with a final design that you're happy with. This is a natural part of the design process and having multiple designs to choose from is a good thing! Alternatively, your initial drawings can be photocopied, cut out and simply placed over your item of clothing to be photographed in many different mock-ups until the best layout has been decided **(Fig. 5.)**.

PREPARING FOR EMBROIDERY

Because this design uses the same illustrations multiple times in different colours and sizes, some of the elements were photocopied at different scales in order to trace them onto water-soluble film

for the embroideries. The dark backgrounds of the patch material could have made it difficult to see the guidelines if this were done in a regular, black pen so a white Posca pen was used instead. The white lines clearly stand out when embroidering and make it easy to follow, giving you the best results **(Fig. 6.)**.

Black felt was sandwiched in between a layer of tear-away backing and the clear topping with the design on it, and pinned in place before framing up in a spring embroidery hoop for tension. Use any embroidery hoop you like, as long as when it's framed up it's the correct way for free-motion, and the fabric touches the table or the base of your sewing machine when in the hoop **(Fig. 7.)**. Pins can sometimes get in the way of the embroidery hoop when stitching, so you may want to trace out the outlines with stitches to secure the three materials together so you can take them out and continue embroidering without being pricked by them **(Fig. 8.)**.

This jacket design is mirrored perfectly on both sides (apart from the sleeves and central back), meaning that a lot of the embroideries must have a perfectly mirrored design on the two shoulder and front pieces and part of the back. This mirror effect is best achieved by using

7

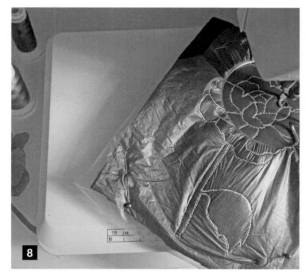

8

9

the same image for both sides and by drawing the outlines onto the water-soluble film and then flipping it upside down for one of the pieces, so that the side that has been drawn on faces the fabric to be embroidered. **(Fig. 9.)**.

When using patches, consider whether you want the extra fabric to act as a feature of its own, or to blend into the garment. On this jacket, the decision was made to intentionally use black felt patch fabric for the embroidered patches, to create a contrasting effect against the pale denim material. For a more subtle look, use the closest colour you can find to your garment for your patch base, and when cutting out your embroidered patches, cut around your embroidery up to one millimetre away from the stitches for the smallest outline without taking away the stability around the embroidery. If you cut too close, even if you don't snip the threads, the stitches can come loose and unravel.

EMBROIDERING THE PATCHES
Decide which order you want to embroider your colours in. Be guided by the order in which you used colour in your drawings, be that paint, pencil, felt

pen or any other medium. Greens are often a good place to start with florals, as they tend to be in the background while the flower is the main feature. Embroidering the less important colours first and the most prominent ones last will make the right sections of the embroidery pop.

The butterflies in this project were embroidered with the lightest colour first and then going up through the shades to end on black for the most impact **(Fig. 10.)**.

Flowers were embroidered with the green colour first and then moving onto the lightest petal colour, and ending on the darker shades. When shading with free-motion embroidery or satin stitch free-motion, it helps to stitch your first colour a little over where you think it should fade out, so that it can be blended in with the next colour **(Fig. 11.)**.

Flowers look beautiful when embroidered using the zig-zag free-motion technique. The satin edges allow the colours to show their full hue, due to the longer stitch lengths involved in this process. When using the zig-zag stitch combined with free-motion embroidery, you will need to move your hands much more slowly so that the satin stitch doesn't leave gaps in the embroidery. You will need to rotate the hoop with your hands to change the direction of the material, in order to get the correct angle for the satin stitch effect **(Fig. 12.)**.

When embroidering the same patch multiple times as with the mirrored florals in this project, it helps to complete them all together – stitching the first colour on both patches before changing to the next colour and so on **(Fig. 13.)**. This cuts out a lot of thread changing and helps to get the pieces looking as uniform or symmetrical as possible. Small changes like thread colour sequence can change the overall look of the embroidery.

Working on coloured backgrounds can save time if that colour is part of your design – just leave gaps where the colour should be, and only stitch with this colour for detail like the large statement butterfly feature on one of the sleeves. The largest butterfly illustration was blown up to almost twice the size of the original drawing to create some very large sections of black within the design. These could

have taken a long time to fill in, even with a zig-zag stitch, but instead they were outlined with black thread during the last step of the embroidery, using a small zig-zag. You can do this with large sections of colour that don't match your background colour, by appliquéing on some additional fabric in your chosen colour and outlining it with a zig-zag to cover any raw edges. Stitch detail over it with free-motion, or leave it blank. Outlining with a different colour or shade can change the effect of the appliquéd fabric too. All these options will create different effects so consider these when designing your embroidery

(Fig. 14.).

APPLYING THE PATCHES

Always remove your backing and topping materials before trimming around your embroidered patches. If the water-soluble film needs soaking in warm water to remove any stubborn areas, allow it to completely dry before ironing, and stitching down onto your garments (Fig. 15.).

If you don't work out your proportions properly when drawing out your design placement (which can be difficult and time consuming), you may find that

the embroideries do not fit together on your garment exactly as planned – this is OK! The design drawings are a guide so if you need to adjust the placements ever so slightly to fit nicely on your item of clothing, then do so. Just make sure you think about any other pieces that need to be added. You can either complete all your embroidered patches first, pinning them in place to make sure they all fit together before stitching down, or appliqué them on as you go along. Just be sure you have enough room for all your pieces if you use this method **(Fig. 16.)**.

Machine stitching an embroidered patch using an appliqué technique onto a ready made garment can be problematic. Some areas may be difficult to get to with your machine and, especially with thicker pieces like denim, parts can be rigid, and the thick seams tough to sew through. You can get pricked by the pins holding the patches in place so, if this bothers you or if your garment is simply too difficult to appliqué the patches on with a machine, it may be best to hand stitch your patches.

Most of the patches on this jacket were hand stitched due to them being over thick seams and in tricky, hard-to-reach areas like the sleeves. Using a

single piece of cotton thread in the same colour as the patch and a hand sewing needle, a few stitches were made on the inside of the garment under the first patch to secure the thread. The needle was then pushed through to the front of the garment, catching the edge of the patch material at the same time, and couching over the edge, bringing the needle back to the front again **(Fig. 17.)**.

This couching technique was repeated all the way around the patch, with approximately 2 millimetres in between each stitch, and finished off with a few more secure stitches on the inside of the garment.

Thick garments like this denim jacket will be tough to hand stitch in some areas, especially the thick seams. Use a fairly thick needle for stitching (definitely don't use a beading needle). If you struggle to get through some areas, use a thimble to push your stitches through **(Fig. 18.)**.

For the few patches that were sewn onto the jacket using a sewing machine, the top and bobbin threads were changed to a black cotton thread (try to avoid using any Sulky, shiny embroidery threads for the application of patches). Sometimes the bobbin thread can show through at the top when

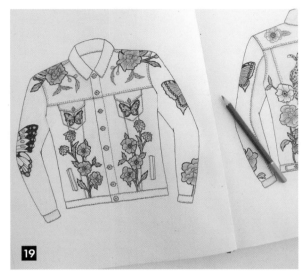

appliquéing, so using the same or similar colour yarn on your bobbin as your top thread will avoid any flecks showing through.

Use the straight foot to attach your patches on a sewing machine, with the machine settings set to a regular zig-zag as described in 'Zig-Zag Sewing' under 'Techniques & Tips' with a medium sized zig-zag width, and approximately two millimetres length. Due to the thickness of the materials, the needle was swapped for a much thicker one – small, thin, 70/10 needles are fantastic for getting detail into your embroideries because of how small the puncture holes they create are. However, they can often break when used for appliquéing, especially when the materials involved are quite dense.

Embroidering Directly onto the Denim Jacket

Although denim is a great material to embroider directly onto (and can even often be done without any stabiliser materials), made up garments like jackets can often come with very dense, heavy areas where many layers of the fabric have been stitched together for seams or feature elements – these areas are impossible to free-motion embroider onto. This fact

influenced the idea to combine patch embroideries with a few directly applied to the garment to create two different effects.

When designing the jacket and creating illustrations of the completed piece, these issues were resolved before the project was started. The decision was made that all the arm pieces which would be difficult to embroider on, and all sections with thick feature seams would have patch embroideries, and all the larger areas that would be easy to access with an embroidery hoop would be direct, on the garment embroideries. To indicate these two types of design on the design illustration, all the patches were drawn with thick, black outlines to represent the dark patch border, and any to be embroidered onto the denim were left with no outline. This clearly indicated the difference between the two and acted as a useful reference when doing the embroidery work **(Fig. 19.)**.

Because the denim in this jacket was very light in colour, the tiger, leopard and any floral motifs that were embroidered directly onto the denim jacket were traced out onto some water-soluble film using a regular, dark coloured ball-point pen for

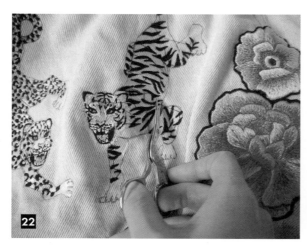

the clearest guidelines. For darker denims, the white Posca pen would have worked best, but in this case a dark outline was required **(Fig. 20.)**.

Normally the black thread would be embroidered last, but in this case, it was done first. Because of the number of stripes and spots on the tiger and leopard, if the black thread was saved until after the base yellows and oranges, there would have been a lot of jump stitches between the shapes to cut out **(Fig. 21.)**.

When cutting away lots of tiny jump stitches over other parts of stitching, it can be easy to accidentally

cut threads that should not be cut. By doing the black first, the yellows and oranges could be stitched around the shapes, covering up the jump stitches in between, and eliminating the need to cut the jump stitches away because they are hidden with more embroidery. If you are left with any particularly long pieces of thread between stitched areas, these should still be cut away **(Fig. 22.)**.

A few small sections of foliage were extended onto the jacket from the patches. These were drawn onto the water-soluble film free hand, using small elements of the coloured illustrations, and mixing them

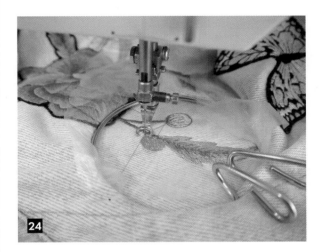

together **(Fig. 23.)**, **(Fig. 24.)**, **(Fig. 25.)**.

The final step for this vibrant, statement denim jacket was to add the text – you can embroider text directly onto your garment, or create a patch first. It can be as personal or as general as you like., The text was designed by drawing the word 'femme' free hand, in a loose, handwritten style. No printouts or stencils were needed **(Fig. 26.)**.

If you want to use text and struggle with handwriting, you can print out your words from a computer and just trace onto your water-soluble film from that.

Because the text was embroidered in white, to avoid any stubborn dark areas around the edges of the wording, it was traced onto the water-soluble film using the same white Posca pen as was used for the patches. This made it more difficult to see, but meant that the edges would be crisp white when completed **(Fig. 27.)**.

This finished jacket is vibrant, eclectic and a complete statement piece, which was the aim throughout the entire design process. Design your garments how you want them to look, express your creativity through your embroidery skills and use

this project as guide to creating beautiful, upcycled garments that will be worn for years to come, or even get passed down through members of your family as heirloom pieces. You need never throw anything away again, just because it's gone out of style, or got a few holes. The beauty of customising your own clothes is that you get to design them for yourself, how you want, to go with clothing you already own, and what better way to show off your skills than to wear them?

TIPS FOR FREE-MOTION PROJECTS

Big projects like this will take a long time and are a huge commitment so keep this in mind. Don't be disheartened if it takes longer than expected - keep going because the finished piece will be worth the effort. The denim jacket in this final project took two months to complete!

When working on free-motion projects with lots of embroidery, you may end up with lots of backing and topping scraps – keep these for smaller projects and more miniature embroideries, it will save some money and avoid more waste.

Animals are one of the hardest things to embroider – they're even difficult to draw. If you struggle with drawing true to life animals, try doing a more stylised version of your chosen animal. Use some patterned fabrics with leopard print or tiger print, and just stitch details like features, shading and highlights to create a quirky, unusual effect.

You can use Thermoweb Peel 'N' Stick Fabric Fuse to apply patches to your garments to save time, however, nothing is as secure as sewing them on. Once you have used Thermoweb Peel 'N' Stick Fabric Fuse do not stitch over the patches as your needles will get covered in adhesive.

If at any point in a big project, you feel like you genuinely like how it's looking, and would rather stop and keep it half done, do so. There were many stages throughout this denim jacket project where the piece looked stunning, and could have been left without continuing to embroider the entire piece. Always keep in mind what the final end result will look like. It is often worth the time and effort.

stockist directory

MATERIALS
Tear Away Backing: www.sewessential.co.uk
Solvy Water Soluble Film:
www.sewessential.co.uk
White Felt Material for Patches:
www.gs-ukdirect.co
Black Felt Material for Patches:
www.gs-ukdirect.com
Fabric Scraps, Felt, Cotton and Denim (if not
already preowned): www.ebay.co.uk
Gold Seed Beads and Emerald Green Crystals:
www.beadsolutions.co.uk
Iron-On Interfacing / Bondaweb:
www.hobbycraft.co.uk
Masking / Washi Tape:
www.hobbycraft.co.uk

EQUPMENT
BERNINA 1008 Classic:
www.bernina.com
BERNINA Extension Table:
www.berninasewingshop.co.uk
BERNINA Freehand Embroidery Foot:
www.berninasewingshop.co.uk
BERNINA Zig Zag (straight) Foot:
www.berninasewingshop.co.uk
BERNINA Size 70 (70/10) Ballpoint Needles:
www.tysew.co.uk
Spring Embroidery Hoop:
www.hobbycraft.co.uk
Kearing Air Erasable Pen:
www.bobbingirl.co.uk
Stork Embroidery Scissors:
www.johnlewis.com
Posca White Marker Pen:
www.hobbycraft.co.uk

Thermoweb Peel N' Stick Fabric Fuse Sheets:
www.barnyarns.co.uk
Beading Needles: www.hobbycraft.co.uk
Hand Sewing Needles:
www.hobbycraft.co.uk
Round Headed Pins: www.hobbycraft.co.uk
Thimble: www.hobbycraft.co.uk

THREADS
Gunold Sulky Embroidery Threads:
www.gs-ukdirect.com
Gunold Cotty Threads:
www.gs-ukdirect.com
Gunold Mety Threads:
www.gs-ukdirect.com
Gunold Poly Threads:
www.gs-ukdirect.com
Gütermann Sulky Rayon Threads:
www.sewessential.co.uk
Gütermann Sew All Threads:
www.sewessential.co.uk
Madeira Rayon Classic Threads:
www.barnyarns.co.uk

**RECOMMENDED PLACES FOR SECOND
HAND CLOTHING**
Local charity shops
www.cancerresearchuk.org
www.onlineshop.oxfam.org.uk
www.barnardos.org.uk

Online pre-loved fashion resale
www.ebay.co.uk
www.depop.com

About the author

Connie Mabbott is an embroidery designer who loves to create vibrant and unique clothing. She sells ethical and sustainable embroidered clothing through her online shop, Connie's World. She also loves to customise pre-loved clothing found in charity vintage shops and online second hand retailers. She grew up in North Wales, and moved to Birmingham to study Embroidered Textile Design at Birmingham City University.

Being brought up in a very rural area of Wales meant that growing up Connie was surrounded by nature. This childhood inspired her love for floral and leafy embroideries. Connie loves fashion and life in the city she now lives in! Embroidery is both her job and her hobby, so time off from her sewing machine is a rare occurrence. However, she also enjoys yoga and returning home to her parent's house in Wales to relax and take a step back from work and that ever whirring sewing machine.

Instagram: @_conniesworld

Acknowledgements My biggest thank you is to my boyfriend, Rhys. He has been there for me throughout the making of this book, cooked for me when I was too busy, helped with photographing some of the hand shots that I couldn't quite capture on my own, and drove me all the way to Bristol for the final shoot. I couldn't have done it without him! To my parents, Julie and Peter, for always being so supportive of me, and encouraging me to follow my chosen career path despite how insecure it can be. To my best friend, Erin, for keeping me sane and for always being there for me at the right time. She has been my cheerleader along the way. And finally to Jesse Wild, the photographer on the main shoot, and Jaine Bevan, the stylist, who made the pieces looks absolutely stunning. They both made me feel at ease on set.